In Performance

EDITED BY
CAROL MARTIN

In Performance is a book series devoted to national and global theater of the twenty-first century. Scholarly essays providing the theatrical, cultural, and political contexts for the plays and performance texts introduce each volume. The texts are written both by established and emerging writers, translated by accomplished translators, and aimed at people who want to put new works on stage, read diverse dramatic and performance literature, and study diverse theatre practices, contexts, and histories in light of globalization.

In Performance has been supported by translation and editing grants from the following organizations:

The Book Institute, Krakow
TEDA Project, Istanbul
The Memorial Fund for Jewish Culture, New York
Polish Cultural Institute, New York
Zbigniew Raszewski Theatrical Institute, Warsaw

Dear
Amy and
Steven,
Warmest wishes
and thanks,
Yasmine

THE WAR ZONE
IS MY BED

AND OTHER PLAYS

Yasmine Beverly Rana

Seagull
BOOKS

LONDON NEW YORK CALCUTTA

Seagull Books 2011

ISBN-13 978 1 9064 9 770 5

British Library Cataloging-in-Publication Data
A catalog record for this book is available from the British Library

Designed by Bishan Samaddar, Seagull Books, Calcutta, India
Printed and bound by Hyam Enterprises, Calcutta, India

CONTENTS

ACKNOWLEDGEMENTS | **vi**

INTRODUCTION | **vii**
Domnica Radulescu

BIBLIOGRAPHY | **xxi**

BLOOD SKY | **1**

RETURNING | **60**

THE WAR ZONE IS MY BED | **103**

PARADISE | **150**

ACKNOWLEDGEMENTS

The author would like to thank the editors of the following who published excerpts from some of the plays featured here:

The Best Women's Stage Monologues of 1999 (Jocelyn A. Beard ed., Hanover: Smith and Kraus, 2001); *The Best Stage Scenes of 1999* (Jocelyn A. Beard and Joanne Genadio ed., Hanover: Smith and Kraus, 2001); *Blackbird* (2005, 2007, available at www.blackbird.vcu.edu/nvr/); *The Kenyon Review* (Winter 2007); *TDR The Drama Review* (Spring 2008); *U.S. 1 Worksheets* (2002).

The theater of Yasmine Beverly Rana is necessary and overpowering. It is necessary because of the urgency of its political engagement and overpowering due to the intensity of its fundamental existential quest and the rawness of the emotions that run through it.

The physical, cultural, and psychological landscapes of this volume are as diverse and haunting: the mythic Deep South of Louisiana alongside the Mississippi (*Blood Sky*); a bedroom in post-Bosnian War Sarajevo or an art gallery in New York in the early 2000s (*Returning*); a bed in a room with blackened windows in Taliban-ridden Kabul (*The War Zone Is My Bed*); a room in Katrina-devastated New Orleans (*Paradise*).

The vibrant diversity of this theater derives its aesthetic and philosophical cohesiveness from a motif that pulsates almost obsessively from one scene to the next, from one play to another. A motif that is most often voiced through persistent questions: What does one find at the very core of a human being in extreme life-and-death situations after she or he has been stripped of every-thing—country, material possessions, family, profession, identity, and even dignity? What does one hold on to and how does one go on after she or he has come out at the other end of war, genocide, dictatorship, childhood trauma, natural catastrophe, loss of loved ones and, in the end, loss of everything other than one's physical body and the ability to think and speak? Woven into this existen-tial query is also a consistent questioning of the role of art itself in the face of unspeakable human pain and violence. Can art save us?

What are the responsibilities of the artist in the face of oppression, violence, injustice? Who is telling whose stories, and does that matter?

Rana's theater achieves a stunning balance between harsh political and cultural realities and profound ontological questions. From her early brooding play *Blood Sky* to the title play *The War Zone Is My Bed*, to the ironically titled *Paradise*, and to *Returning*, the reader or the spectator makes an unsettling, exhilarating, and enriching journey through a poetic universe of battling wills and haunting voices that—set against the background of dark and unforgiving historical, familial, and natural violence—cry out in a desperate need for survival. These battles of wills are sometimes woven with raw sexualities; and, as such, one of the spaces or objects of predilection that keeps reappearing in the last three plays of the collection is the very basic and primal bed—a place not only of ultimate intimacy but also of raw vulnerabilities and shared despair.

The first play of the volume, *Blood Sky*, is as shocking and fantastical as its title declares it to be. In the tradition of some of the best Southern literature—reminiscent of William Faulkner or Tennessee Williams—the play envelops us with its sultry, smoldering atmosphere where the oppressive heat and the lull of the Mississippi become metaphors for disturbing sexualities, dark childhood traumas, and unquenched yearnings. In a brilliant theatrical discovery, Rana builds around her female protagonist Joley a mesmerizing game of multiple identities, each of which is an incarnation of a different time in the character's life: The 14-year-old rebellious and angry Joley; the 18-year-old Joley painfully coming into her womanhood with jagged hopes of romance; and the mature 30-year-old Joley who is the unifying conscience and the narrator of all the Joleys, including the 6-year-old girl whose terrifying trauma lurks unforgivingly in all of them.

The plot moves back and forth among the three main stages in Joley's life, and unfolds the three temporal threads almost simultaneously with several arresting scenes in which either two or all three of the Joleys come together on stage and enter into dialogue, expressing a constant need to understand and explore, to repair and forgive, to gain meaning and guidance from each other across time, space and experience. The unconventional and non-naturalistic theatrical device of splitting one character into several different voices, ages, personas, actually adds a phenomenological depth to the representation of time. The audience often sees the past and the present merge or converse with each other, thus gaining a deeper understanding of the ways in which past actions have consequences in the present and how the present mirrors both the traumas one experienced and the choices one made in the past.

Powerful examples include the scene in the beginning of the play when Joley 30 asks Joley 18 to tell Stone, the latter's boyfriend, the truth about her past relationship; and the scenes in which Joley 30 emerges right next to Joley 14 and starts to recount key moments from her childhood and early adolescence, such as the frightening night of the 6-year-old Joley who, left alone with her mother's boyfriend Bo, is terrified of or actually experiences the "bad" that is so terrible that "you can't even say it out aloud," and the account of her mother's transition from boyfriends to "finding God," and joining a church "to ease her guilt."

Scenes between Joley 14 and an uncanny male character called Guy, always dressed in immaculate white, are interwoven with scenes between Joley 18 and a young man called Stone and scenes in which Joley 30 casts light on the past through her monologues, and, further, interspersed with scenes in which Joley 14 either confronts her mother Lily or is harassed by a group of neighborhood boys. Toward the end of Act II, the three Joleys come together and the play ends with them listening, looking at the fire-colored blood sky and vowing to "overpower" the "bad," the dark secret, the scary place in their memory, their subconscious, and their past, which has haunted and tormented them/her throughout their/her life. The spaces where the scenes of the play take place are arche-typal, all-American, brooding. They echo unspeakable secrets, reek of blood and illicit actions, even with shadows of Tom Sawyer and Huck Finn: A road, a car at the roadside, a fence, a river, the front porch of a house, always framed by a red, ominous sky. The story does actually have a Tom-and-Huck duo turned bad—the two boys, Ray and Jo-Jo, who, having once mocked and harassed Joley, are found to have drowned in the river. Their bodies are discovered tied to a raft mysteriously with the barbed wire from the fence in front of Joley's house, a deed most likely performed by the impec-cably clean, white, and chilling Guy:

> JOLEY 14. Hot. Summer. Darkness. Quiet. Too quiet. Ma. Bo. Blood. Bloody sheets. Boys. Stupid boys . . .
>
> JOLEY 18. Huck and Tom on crack.

Pulsing through every scene in a continuous line as red as the ominous sky looming in the background are the anguish, the desire, the pain, the hope of women who have been hurt, deserted, artificially "protected," sometimes thrilled but most often disappointed by the men in their lives. Lily, the mother, vents her anger at being deserted, at having to do it all, at the condition of single motherhood, and, at times, at Joley herself. The confronta-tions between mother and daughter are strained and they speak as much of the confusion and pain of each of them as they do of the tension between them. The childhood trauma that Joley carries with her throughout the stages of her life is at the source of all her pain, confusion, and the split in her identity. The loneliness, the sense of not belonging, the self stripped of identity—these are all theatrical elements present in incipient form in this early play; they are developed more turbulently in the later ones. *Blood Sky* is troubling as it is beautifully and broodingly crafted, both in terms of imagery and development of character. It touches us where our deepest fears and darkest memories lurk and ask for appeasement.

The War Zone Is My Bed is the centerpiece of this collection, with the iconic bed as the critical space where all confrontations, dialogues, silences, and emotions unfold. The bed is also the space of storytelling, of stories by or of women living through oppression, violence, and atrocities—the Bosnian War and the Taliban regime in Afghanistan. The locations vary from Sarajevo to Kabul to New York to Dubrovnik. The central story is that of Laila from Part 2 of the play, a woman trying to survive the most atrocious times under the Taliban by living in a room with blackened windows and working secretly as a prostitute. She is eventually executed like so many others, under the eyes of men, including her own lover, Ash. Most of the other scenes in the play are about the different ways in which her story is recorded, transmitted, and transfigured. Laila's story is passed on to Dahlia, a writer and a native of Sarajevo, from Ash whom she interviews in Part 3, also in an apartment in Kabul. In Part 1, Dahlia is in confrontation with Peter, a journalist writing a book about the recent Bosnian War with Dahlia's story in it. Then there is Susan, Peter's wife, in Part 4, whom Peter found at the moment of her being hit by a car and turned into "a spectacle," unconscious in the middle of the street. In Part 5, Dahlia and the Bosnian journalist Tony are also in bed, exchanging stories, talking about "documenting trauma" and, in the end, discussing Dahlia's manuscript of the story of Laila and Ash. In Part 6 we return—full circle—to the characters of Peter and Dahlia from Part 1, this time in a New York bookstore, on the occasion of the launch of Dahlia's book.

The play is as much about the stories of Laila, Dahlia, Susan, their traumas, their suffering, their courage to face danger, pain and even violent death, and their relations to male lovers, as it is about "documenting trauma," the transformation of traumatic experiences into art, the transmission or appropriation of stories. It is about the need to testify and tell the stories of women like Laila, women who blackened their windows and gave themselves to strangers in order to survive, who were silenced brutally and unjustly and yet had the courage to love and live and, eventually, to embrace the terrible consequences of "un-blackening" their windows. It is about women like Dahlia who, despite surviving war and bombs and misery and "grime", appropriate the stories of others even more desperate and hopeless. "We collect people. We can't help it. We can't disregard them, so they become a part of us. She's a part of me now. So is he," says Dahlia to her lover in Dubrovnik, and her words apply to the rest of the characters, as their destinies become entangled uncannily with one another through not only the act of storytelling but also the intimacy of sex. In the worst of times, people embrace each other in a desperate need for warmth and closeness and tell stories in a need for remembrance. One scene after another, the play beautifully knits the characters' fates—their tears, their silences, their cries for help—into a complex tapestry in which we see the transformation of human experience into art under our very eyes: a startling simultaneity between the lived experience and its sublimation into the words that retell it. The most poignant of these threads is the story of Laila. It is first lived/acted directly in front of the audience in the scene with Ash, then becomes the interview between Dahlia and Ash, which is then read and discussed by Tony, and, eventually, becomes the book that brings Dahlia and Peter face to face again in the end. What happens to Laila's story? It becomes not only

Dahlia's story, or Tony's, or Peter's, but ours as well. We have processed the story in its many avatars in our hearts and minds, we have hoped for it to turn out differently, we have hoped for some redemption and have learned that if there is any, it is only in our own gesture of taking Laila's story with us and making it our own.

Returning is an exquisitely crafted play that poses some of the most urgent question of our times: What are the ethical responsibilities and parameters of art that testifies to historical violence and atrocities? What is the ultimate purpose or benefit, if any, of testifying to historical atrocities through art? How do survivors of atrocities actually survive? How do those who witnessed atrocities make sense of their stories and of what they have witnessed? As in the other plays in the volume, we see history, politics, war, genocide unfold through the direct experiences of individuals, in their most intimate settings and situations, in the rawness of sexual encounters, confessions, and art-making. *Returning* is also a play about "trauma tourism"—deliberately going back to the place of one's trauma. This mythic movement of the return is also what guides the play's concentric dramatic construction of stories embedded within stories.

We are faced here with the intriguing notion of selling stories, of exchanging life stories, and of entanglement of stories to the point where the characters' narratives and identities become inseparable. In the opening scene, Azra, a native of Sarajevo, visits Rania, an asylum-seeker from Afghanistan, at a detention center in New York. The story of a woman losing everything under the rule of the Taliban—her work, her identity, her husband, her children—acquires a life of its own in this commerce of stories. The characters' individual lives become indistinguishable from each other and all we are left with in this troubling theatrical moment is the image of two women exchanging stories of grief, becoming each other

and melting into each other's grief. Rania articulates this entanglement in a strikingly beautiful image:

> Her story was my story. Husband and children? I think I had
> at one time, but no more. So all the stories become rooted
> into one thick tree trunk. And we become entangled inside
> the branches until no one can distinguish one from the
> other. And her rings on that trunk, become my rings.
> They're ours, and now . . . they're yours!

In the next scene, we see Azra with Marco—also a native of
Sarajevo, a student, and a photographer—as they exchange stories
in bed about the Sniper Avenue massacre during the Bosnian War.
The photographs that Marco took during the massacre stare at
them unforgivingly from the wall. Azra has heard of the incident
from other people, including her friend Jasna who had been
raped by soldiers and had wanted to kill herself but could not,
and, of course, her lover Marco who was present at the scene of
the heinous crime, taking photographs. Azra accumulated other
people's stories of violence and terror to cope with her own guilt
for having been absent from the scene, living safely in America
during the atrocities in her country. She has to keep inventing and
reinventing herself to give meaning to her absence:

> I stopped. I stepped back. I rewrote my own history . . .
> which I think is a rather extraordinary thing to do . . . ridding
> people, silencing yourself, so, perhaps, we're left to think that
> we were imagined, that there was never an "us." We were
> never born, so we never died. We never were. I could won-
> der, but I couldn't say it aloud. Then it would be real.

In the next scene that takes place in an art gallery in Sarajevo,
Marco has to confront Andrea, a woman whose husband and
daughter both died in the massacre on Sniper Avenue. As she walks
around the exhibition we feel the unbearable burden of her pain,

the pain of mourning mothers and widows of all times—Hecubas and Andromaches. She is angered by the photographs, and questions Marco's morality for making art, making money, and acquiring fame through photographs that capture unspeakable human suffering, her own suffering, which is still raw, still real, not sublimated—nor can it ever be—into art. Slowly, in the telling of her story though, she starts to understand Marco and his need to capture the event:

> I went out, out to the avenue, and there was another man; a photographer, like you. He was there, but he wasn't shot. Just like I wasn't shot. He pulled out his camera, and right next to me, in crossfire, started taking pictures, one after the other, so intently [. . .] It seemed so . . . wrong. It was as if we were breaking some very sacred rule . . . this deep intrusion into something so sacred, and so intimate. I shouldn't have stopped him. Maybe he saw them through his lens, and I might have had something left . . . something I could have kept. Maybe I do understand you now.

In the heart-wrenching contact with the memory of her trauma through Marco's photograph, Andrea is ultimately wistful for not being able to find even a trace of her lost loved ones in the very photographs that she first rejected.

Caroline, a young woman present in Sarajevo on Sniper Avenue, tells her story to the technician performing her breast sonogram. She narrates the story of Andrea, the woman who lost her husband and daughter on Sniper Avenue. Caroline admits she felt more alive than ever in the midst of the shooting and the violence: "I got hooked. I wasn't afraid of anything, you see. Nothing shook me. Affected me, yes, but didn't frighten me. [. . .] I never got sick. I never got shot. I never got lonely. I never got scared." This is ironic, as we see her now nervously following the technician's every move and expression. She is anxious, afraid.

The play ends with the poignant encounter between Azra, the native of Sarajevo, who was not "there" when it happened, and Caroline, who was. Each asks of each other and of themselves whether it mattered that they were there or that they were not. Where is home? Was it all for nothing? Are the people in the picture, who are being shot, nothing? Does it make a difference, does it mean anything that both of them are encountering each other and their "home" in the moment captured on camera and exhibited on the wall of an art gallery in New York? Azra is faced with guilt, while Caroline is faced with longing for the place where she experienced both horror and enlightenment. Marco plans to return to Sarajevo. Maybe Azra will too. The play focuses on the way people return to the places of their trauma, to experience them after they have survived them, or, like Azra, to vicariously live the trauma of others in order to expiate for guilt of their own absence. How do people who have survived events such as those on Sniper Avenue continue to give meaning to their experience and to their lives? Does the artist who captures or documents trauma profit from human suffering or does he keep the memory of trauma alive? There are no clear-cut answers to these difficult questions posed by the play. However, from the almost magical way in which people's lives and stories become part of one another, from the telling and retelling of the same stories from different perspectives—that of the victims, the survivors, the witnesses, the story-sellers, and those who helped the victims and survivors—one answer does emerge. It is an answer that unfolds and unwinds like the circles on the tree that Rania talks about: the stubborn need to keep telling the stories of violence, to speak of one's grief, to not keep silent, to document, to become involved in other people's lives and to care, even if for a brief moment, to become the tree on which the stories are being strung, one after another. Because the alternative—that of silence and of *not* telling those stories—is simply not acceptable.

Paradise, a play that returns partly and obliquely to the banks of the Mississippi in Katrina-devastated New Orleans, is a hymn to the most intense form of human despair: the ironic opposite of its title—a woman's Dantesque hell. It is a dark play, but so sublimely tragic that in it the darkness itself shines. Meena is stoned to death in an honor killing because of her love for Raj and her sexual relationship with him. In the shocking first scene, Meena tells her gruesome story of violent death from inside her grave, while sifting stones and pebbles with her fingers. Echoes of great sacrificial victims and tragic heroines from classical literature and myth reverberate through Meena's opening monologue— Iphigenias, Antigones, Persephones. Meena's voice allies itself to the ageless voice of women crying out against their violent immolations in the name of inhumane principles and laws devised by patriarchal societies, societies that have always had to legitimize their arbitrary power by resorting to what René Girard called the sacrifice of a scapegoat in order to keep intact the order and "purity" of a community.

> But here I am, under the pebbles, under the sand, without light, without breath, with a name, with a place, without honor, with shame. Shame for having loved you, more than I or you, or anyone could understand. With air and time running out, here I stand. A citizen, with shame, self-imposed shame, they say. On my knees, face to the ground, mouth in the dirt, skin torn by pebbles and shards of glass, tossed into my grave, dug by my hands, my nails, myself. All for love? Honor? Shame? Stripped of citizenship and home, and buried without a name. [. . .] Look at what you've saved me from—all that! Thank you.

Paradise is constructed in a wrenching back-and-forth movement between the past of Meena's interrogation and trial, the present of her death, the past of her love with Raj in a room in their country, the past "hell" of the trial again, the "happy" interlude—"paradise"—with Raj in a gradually flooding apartment in New Orleans two days after Hurricane Katrina. The characters are phantoms—humans reduced to their most naked vulnerability and essential humanity in a nerve-wrenching confrontation reminiscent of Jean-Paul Sartre's *No Exit* (1944). The flooded apartment is their hell and their redemption, their refuge and their tomb. The readers/spectators are vicarious participants in the strained and tragic intimacy of these two characters as they battle with each other and with the world, as they desperately cling to survival and to each other, two illegal refugees in a flooded city or two illegal lovers in a terrifying country trying to escape. The unusual construction of the plot starts with Meena speaking from inside her grave, then moves backwards in time by throwing us into their past, to the beginnings of their relationship in their own country, then to their refuge apartment in New Orleans, back to the interrogation of Meena, startlingly conducted by Raj himself who moves back and forth in the double role. This orchestration creates a sense of moral and emotional vertigo: we follow the free fall of these desperate people, but mostly of Meena herself—through atrocity, natural disaster, inefficient government, deportation, and, finally, immolation. Flood-ravaged New Orleans is, ironically, the high point in the characters' tortuous journey: the room from where Meena eventually escapes (only to be deported to her own country), the room in which Raj dies as the building is swept away by the flood. Their paradise is, in fact, the lighter of the circles of hell into which they descend rapidly, much like the souls in Dante's *Inferno*—two modern Asian Francesca da Rimini and Paolo Malatesta, subjected to crueler laws in our twenty-first century than in Dante's Middle Ages. As she descends into the hell, Meena's fierce courage—to love and live with utmost intensity despite everything until nothing but her bare soul and immolated body are left—rises, moves in the opposite direction: a stubborn and excruciating voice ascending, clinging, climbing, refusing to be silenced even after death.

In the urgency of its political message, in its uncompromising feminism, in the depth of its existential questions, in the exquisite framing of stories and in the composition of characters who tell or live them—all incarnated in sensuous and hauntingly poetic language—Yasmine Beverly Rana's dramatic work is one that has made, and will continue to make, its mark not only on the history of theater and aesthetics but also on society and on the lives of women. This is theater at its best, theater that our world could not and should not do without, theater that denounces and resists injustice, theater that brings the bodies, voices, experiences of women centerstage, theater in which the most diverse and powerful of human emotions and the most sophisticated of intellectual ideas merge in language that quivers with subtle nuance, varied tonalities, and vibrantly dark colors.

The voices and gestures of Laila, Joley, Meena, Azra, Rania, Andrea, Dahlia, Susan, and Caroline stay with us long after the last words of these plays have been uttered. Blackening and unblackening windows, sifting through pebbles in a grave, writing, telling, crying out one's stories, being subjected to cruel interrogations, whispering words of love, shouting words of anger—these gestures and voices speak of and touch something primitive, sacred, almost cruelly intimate in most of us, a raw human feeling that connects us to each other and to ancient, mythic female figures. But at the same time, in its modern execution and the consistent questioning of the function of art itself, in the levels of self-subversion created by the artist figures in the plays—from Joley the storyteller to Dahlia the writer to Tony the journalist to Marco the photographer to Rania the story-seller—in the deliberate fragmentation and concentricity of narratives, and the unconventional, even unsettling, representation of time, Rana's theatre also stands as fully modern. She creates a genre fully her own, with a strong hold in postmodernity that makes the questions she poses and the emotions she voices even more vibrant, even more transformative, and even more impossible to escape.

ALIGHIERI, Dante. 1995. *The Divine Comedy*. Translated by Allen Mandelbaum. New York: Everyman's Library.

CALINESCU, Matei. 1987. *Five Faces of Modernity: Modernism, Avant-garde, Decadence, Kitsch, Postmodernism*. Durham: Duke University Press.

EURIPIDES. 1955. *The Complete Greek Tragedies*. Translated by David Greene and Richard Lattimore. Chicago: University of Chicago University Press.

GIRARD, René. 1979. *Violence and the Sacred*. Translated by Patrick Gregory. Baltimore: Johns Hopkins University Press.

LAUGHLIN, Louise Karen, and Catherine Schuler. 1995. *Theater and Feminist Aesthetics*. Madison: Fairleigh Dickinson University Press.

LORAUX, Nicole. 1987. *Tragic Ways of Killing a Woman*. Translated by Anthony Forster. Cambridge, MA: Harvard University Press.

———. 1998. *Mothers in Mourning*. Translated by Corinne Pache. Ithaca: Cornell University Press.

RAFFO, Heather. 2007. *Nine Parts of Desire*. Evanston: Northwestern University Press.

STIGLMAYER, Alexandra. 1994. *Mass Rape: The War Against Women in Bosnia-Herzegovina*. Lincoln: University of Nebraska Press.

VISNIEC, Matei. 2002. *The Body of a Woman as Battlefield in the Bosnian War*. In Chreyl Robson (ed.), *Balkan Plots: New Plays from Central and Eastern Europe*. New York: Aurora Metro Press.

WILLIAMS, Tennessee. 1990. *The Theater of Tennessee Williams*. New York: New Directions.

CHARACTERS

JOLEY	Female portrayed at three stages of her life: 14, 18, and 30
STONE	Male, 19
GUY	Male, in his 30s
LILY	Joley's mother, in her 30s
RAY and JO-JO	Males, 17

SETTINGS

The rural American South by the Mississippi River

A dark roadside

The front porch of young Joley's home

A swamp

IMAGE 1.1 *Blood Sky*

Promotional image used for *Blood Sky* premiere.
The Looking Glass Theatre, New York, October 30, 2003.
Photograph by Dennis Dalelio.

BLOOD SKY

Blood Sky premiered at the Looking Glass Theatre, New York, on October 30, 2003, with the following cast and crew:

Joley 14	Erin Scanlon
Joley 18	Charlotte Purser
Joley 30	Rachel Scott
Stone	Akiva Saltzman
Guy	Troy Acree
Lily	Erica Engstrom
Ray	Danny LeGare
Jo-Jo	John Williams

Assistant Directors	Lila Rose Kaplan
	Caroline Reddick Lawson
Production Assistants	B. Clara Kim
	Jennifer Semidey
Set Designer	Matt Downs McAdon
Lighting Designer	Danielle Colburn
Costume Designer	Erica Frank
Sound Designer	Kenneth Nowell
Fight Choreographer	Ian Marshall
Director	Justine Lambert

Summer night. Rural roadside. Joley 30 speaks to the audience.

JOLEY 30. We were driving down this dark road leading to nowhere one night. Me and this guy . . . boy . . . person . . . whatever I met somewhere along the road. It was the summer I left home. Left? Why? Why then? At that moment? "Oh, it was just time to," some may say. Don't buy it. Sometimes it takes just one action, one event, one sentence, one phrase, one word, that overtakes your mobility, and carries you upstairs, to your room, where you open your closet, and pack that one little bag, and walk back down those stairs and out that door—without question—into a night like this one, with me and this . . . guy. Steaming hot. You know, the kind of hot that overwhelms your whole body. It's the kind of hot you experienced as a child when you were sick with a fever, and you would just lie still, and stare into the dark, and listen to the stillness pounding so hard into your head that it almost made you mad. Remember how you couldn't escape from that stillness? Every creak and tear sounded like a never-ending piercing scream. Well that's how that night was. With me and this . . . guy. Music up. Windows down. Dust left behind. Tire tracks pressed hard into the ground. He was driving so fast. And I looked out of my window, into the sky. And the sky was blood red. I swear to you. I had never seen anything like that before. It was like the sky was leading us to the middle of nowhere. It wasn't taking us to Hell. Hell would have been easier to define. It wouldn't have been so frightening because it's something you understand. Hell's a concept you were taught as a child. It was a hanging threat drilled into your head by some traveling preacher in some dust-filled church hall in that little town you spent seventeen years trying to escape from. You would know what to expect from Hell. It would be bad, but not surprisingly bad. You wouldn't have to worry. Your expectations would most definitely be met. You know Hell. But this sky . . . place . . . wasn't Hell. It was more terrifying. Unknown. No man's land. A wasteland. I don't really remember where exactly we were coming from, or what we had done before. It doesn't matter. But I didn't know why the sky was like that. I remember looking for some break. Some blue or black or gray. But there was no relief, just blood, everywhere. And this sky overwhelmed my mind and body in such a way that I asked him to stop the car. I told him we had to. I thought and truly felt the whole world was on fire, and it would soon catch up with us. No matter how fast or how far we drove, this "blood sky" would find us. It would know our whereabouts, where we were coming from, where we were going. It would always be there, waiting for us to get tired of running, and therefore give up. It would win. He laughed and told me I was crazy. This guy wanted me to explain. I couldn't put it into words. It's just that I felt something so horrible, so treacherous. You know when something is so bad you can't explain it. You can't even say it out aloud, because you're afraid once it's said, it'll happen.

The past. Night. Lights up on Stone leaning against an old car. Joley 18 joins him.

JOLEY 18. I love you.

STONE. Don't say things you don't mean.

JOLEY 18. But I do mean it.

STONE. We're strangers to each other. How long have we known each other? Barely a week? You have no idea if I've been telling lies or telling truths. You know nothing about me. Not even my name.

JOLEY 18. Fine. You win. Then I don't love you.

STONE. So why'd you say it?

JOLEY 18. I enjoyed what we were doing. And what you were doing, and how that made me feel.

STONE. You give out "I love yous" to guys for just touching you?

JOLEY 18. It felt good, OK? What do those words mean anyway? Maybe nothing. So what would it matter if I said it—barely a week later? Nothing! As if I said it barely a week before! Nothing! See?

STONE. You say it too easily. If some guy puts his arms around you or shoves his fingers into you, you probably tell him you love him. You're such a child. How old are you anyway? Fifteen?

JOLEY 18. Eighteen.

STONE. You look twelve. You fall for it too easily. I can see it now. Better watch out. Don't want to get hurt.

JOLEY 18 (*to audience*). You're right. Of course I don't love you. How could I? I don't even like you. You stupid fuck. Okay, I do say those words a lot. But I don't mean them. At least I don't think I do. I'm sure I don't. I've never understood their true meaning. If there is any. I just like saying them. It goes something like this. I need to hear it. You could keep your expression, sincerity, and your tone. For me, "I love you" could be said by anybody or anything, and it would suit me just fine. What it all comes down to is, somebody in the room has to say it. Even if it's me. Even if no one is listening. It just has to be said.

STONE. Close your eyes. Shut out the night, and go to sleep.

JOLEY 18. I can't.

STONE. Afraid of the dark?

JOLEY 18. Doesn't the sky look strange to you?

STONE. No.

JOLEY 18. Did you even look?

STONE. Don't have to.

JOLEY 18. Do you look at anything?

STONE. Do you ever stop talking?

JOLEY 18. No.

STONE (*to Joley 18*). I don't see anything worth looking at.

JOLEY 18. Everything is.

STONE. Maybe I've seen enough.

JOLEY 18. I've probably seen more.

STONE. Is this a contest?

JOLEY 18. The truth.

STONE. Go first, then.

JOLEY 18 (*anxious*). Night's too long, you know. It was worse when I was a kid. I thought it was endless, and it would never be light again. And I would stay up and wait for it to be tomorrow, when everything would be fresh, bright, and forgotten. But night's when you see things, and hear things, when it's supposed to be too dark to look or to listen.

STONE. So what did you see?

Lights slowly turn from Joley 18 and Stone toward Joley 30.

JOLEY 30 (*to audience*). I used to live around here. Before I left and picked up with that one and his heap of crap he called his pride and glory. He truly believed that his car was the only thing in the world he could depend on. Don't worry. It didn't last long. Neither did his car. He was right. I didn't know shit. And I did look like I was twelve. But he was also wrong. I did remember his name—Stone. But he couldn't remember mine, or he didn't care to. And despite that, he has been able to keep his righteous place in my head, because he won it. He challenged me, with his "contest" and took me back that night, without even realizing it. He did it. He broke that silence . . . my silence.

The past. It is day. The bright sun is on Joley 14 who is in the middle of the stage. She closes her eyes, and looks straight into the sun. Lights are up on the rest of the stage. Joley 14 stands behind a waist-high wire fence. We hear an offstage voice.

GUY. You'll blind your eyes that way.

Joley 14 quickly turns to Guy; he is immaculately dressed in white.

JOLEY 14. My eyes were closed.

GUY. Light's stronger. It shoots straight inside you.

JOLEY 14. How do you know?

GUY. I know a lot of things.

IMAGE 1.2 **Joley remembers the day Guy entered her life.**

Rachel Scott as Joley 30, Erin Scanlon as Joley 14, and Troy Acree as Guy.
Blood Sky, Looking Glass Theatre, New York, October 30, 2003.
Photograph by Tony Knight Hawk.

JOLEY 14. Such as?

GUY. Such as, I think you should be in school.

JOLEY 14. School's out. Summer break. Don't you know that?

GUY. Once you're out of school, everything becomes one long blur. Things like Christmas and Saturdays and summer all get lumped together.

JOLEY 14. Where are you from?

GUY. Same place you are.

JOLEY 14. I don't think so.

GUY. Why?

JOLEY 14. 'Cause I'd remember you. You're not from around here.

GUY. I am now.

JOLEY 14. Where are you headed?

GUY. River?

JOLEY 14. Why? It stinks!

GUY. Couldn't tell. That pretty cologne you're wearing covers it all up.

JOLEY 14. That's why I wear it. To cover up this place. This river. Just 'cause I live in it doesn't mean I'm a part of it. Or that it's a part of me. I'm not a part of this place at all.

GUY. You don't belong here?

JOLEY 14. No.

GUY. Where do you belong?

JOLEY 14. Not here. You better get going. I'm not supposed to talk to strangers.

GUY. You seem real calm.

JOLEY 14. I do. But wouldn't want to cause you trouble.

GUY. How would you do that?

JOLEY 14. Just talking to you.

GUY. How old are you anyway? Twelve?

JOLEY 14. Almost fifteen.

GUY. You look younger. Anyone tell you that?

JOLEY 14. Everyone.

GUY. But you talk older.

JOLEY 14. I know.

GUY. Must be difficult fitting in, especially around here, with such maturity. I mean, the other girls your age don't have such an old spirit. They must really bore you. I can understand the difficulty of being set apart.

JOLEY 14. I don't have friends. Not real ones. So I don't have to worry about "fitting" anywhere. Lucky me. I don't feel like talking anymore. (*Steps away from the fence.*)

Guy blocks her way.

GUY. Did I say something wrong?

JOLEY 14 (*slightly nervous*). No. I just have a lot of things to do at home.

GUY (*stepping aside*). OK, Joley.

JOLEY 14. How did you know my name?

GUY. I know a lot of things, remember?

JOLEY 14. How do you know?

GUY (*extending his hand*). I'm Guy.

JOLEY 14. I don't care. How did you know?

GUY. Who are you waiting for?

JOLEY 14. I'm not waiting for anyone!

GUY. Sure you are. At school. Three o'clock. Bell rings. Kids run. Packed together. Groups pile into cars. Laughing. Acting silly. Music up. Windows down. And then they drive off. But you don't. You sit and wait and watch. Hasn't anyone ever asked you to join them, Joley? I'm sure they have. They must. But you just sit on those school steps, and wait, but no one comes. Who are you waiting for?

JOLEY 14. I've never seen you before.

GUY. You've never looked for me before.

JOLEY 14. You can see everything?

GUY. What's there for me to see, Joley? Something you don't want me to see?

JOLEY 14. But I haven't done anything wrong.

GUY. Nothing to worry about then. (*Beat.*) I stand, just like I'm standing now. Behind that big, tall fence they have over there. But this one is better. I like this one. It isn't as divisive. I don't "do" anything. Just watch, and listen.

JOLEY 14. Who else do you watch?

GUY. No one. Just you.

JOLEY 14 (*almost tearful*). Why?

GUY. Because no one else is watching you. That's why.

JOLEY 14. Let me go.

Guy steps aside.

GUY. But I'm here, Joley. And I've been here . . . for days . . . weeks.

JOLEY 14 (*whispering*). Please leave.

GUY. You don't have to look anymore.

Joley 14 leans over the fence, the wire sticking into her body. Lights go down on Guy.

LILY. What are you doing?

Joley 14 quickly turns to her mother, Lily.

JOLEY 14. I was just leaving.

LILY. I just asked you to do one little thing for me! You know I gotta customer waiting at home! Can't wash her hair out without conditioner! Now that you're outta school, I expect you to do more of your share around this place!

JOLEY 14. I do enough.

LILY. How? By giving me lip? Just like your father. Look like him, act like him . . . lazy . . . always expecting more than you'll ever get. Learn early. Don't expect anything! From anyone!

JOLEY 14 (*coolly*). I don't.

LILY (*quietly*). Good. Go on, now.

Joley 14 is still shaken from Guy.

LILY (*continuing*). Turned into a pillar of salt or something? What's the matter?

JOLEY 14. You wouldn't care.

LILY. Right, because I'm such a lousy mother? I'm so lousy and uncaring that I'm working my tail off for you . . . without any help from your old man!

JOLEY 14. It's not my fault.

LILY. Isn't it? (*Beat.*) Just get going. I need that stuff for Ms. Hanley. She's waiting.

Lily leaves Joley 14 standing over the fence. The lights move from Joley 14 to Stone and Joley 18 on the roadside.

STONE. Who were you waiting for?

JOLEY 18. When?

STONE. The first night.

JOLEY 18. No on.

STONE. Could have fooled me.

JOLEY 18. What made you think I was waiting for someone?

STONE. I don't know . . . You were sitting there . . . at the bar . . . alone looking up . . . turning around to see every person who entered the place. Looking at them, then looking away. You were kind of, I don't know, down. Like you were expecting someone, but he never showed.

JOLEY 18. There was no one.

STONE. Or running from him.

JOLEY 18. There was no one.

STONE (*turning away in disbelief*). Whatever.

JOLEY 18. There wasn't.

STONE. I really don't care.

JOLEY 18. I know you don't.

STONE. Good, because that's not what this is about.

Joley 30 stands before Joley 18.

JOLEY 30 (*to Joley 18*). Tell him.

JOLEY 18. No.

JOLEY 30. But there was someone else.

JOLEY 18. Pure protection.

JOLEY 30. Like if you say it out loud, it'll happen.

JOLEY 18. Something like that.

JOLEY 30. But it already happened. You think you're protecting yourself from the "elements." But then after all that effort you put into keeping up your guard, you let the wrong person in. And you regret it, because that mistake you made when you were so vulnerable spoils it for the others you'll isolate. Those who don't deserve it.

JOLEY 18 (*pointing to Stone*). This one does.

The lights go down on Joley 30 and Joley 18. Lights up on Joley 14. She is waiting on the porch steps. It is early evening. We hear whistling. Joley 14 remains, as Guy approaches her.

GUY. Evening.

JOLEY 14. You better get outta here!

GUY. Why? Not allowed to have friends over?

JOLEY 14. We're not friends.

GUY. Not yet. (*Leans over the porch. Joley 14 is paralyzed.*)

JOLEY 14. My ma'll get angry if she sees you.

GUY. She isn't here.

JOLEY 14 (*nervously*). Yes, she is.

GUY (*amused*). No, Joley. We know she isn't.

JOLEY 14. How did you know?

GUY. I waited and watched. She left. And by the looks of things, it could be a long time before she returns. Your ma looked like she couldn't wait to leave.

JOLEY 14. You were in the fields?

GUY. That's right. Very peaceful out there, in the middle of no place. Grass . . . high . . . touching above your knees. Sweet smell. You know the smell of grass after the rain. The only sounds were of crickets and other odd creatures. The rest was quiet. There was almost something spiritual about being out there, and watching this house.

JOLEY 14. I could go straight inside, and lock the door, and call the police!

GUY. I'm sure you could do anything you wanted but there's no need to do that. Or else you would have done that already. And why disturb the authorities? What have I done to you, Joley? I haven't placed a finger on you. I haven't even said any mean things to you. Just nice ones. So why would you do that?

JOLEY 14 (*quietly*). I guess I wouldn't. There's no need. Not yet.

GUY. Not ever.

JOLEY 14. What kind of name is "Guy" anyway?

GUY. Mine.

JOLEY 14. It's strange.

GUY. How?

JOLEY 14. Like, it's not real, you know. A "Guy" is just a guy or man, or boy. Not a real person.

GUY. So what's standing before your eyes? A ghost? Some spirit from the other world? Or a figment of your oh-so-wild-and-creative imagination?

JOLEY 14. That's not what I meant.

GUY. Tell me, then.

JOLEY 14. If I see before me a real man, that real man has some bills to pay. Translation: a job for most of us!

GUY. You don't work.

JOLEY 14. Like hell I don't. I gotta help my ma around here. She cuts hair and gives perms to some ladies around. I gotta do what she says. Clean up. Go to the store. Stuff like that.

GUY. You should just be having fun. Going to parties. Shopping. Meeting fellows.

JOLEY 14. I do. Sometimes.

GUY. Glad to hear it.

JOLEY 14. And what do you do?

GUY. Nothing gets past you.

JOLEY 14. Not usually.

GUY. Well, I do a little of this, a little of that. I'm what you call "freelance."

JOLEY 14. Freelance what?

GUY. Business, buying, selling.

JOLEY 14. That's what you're doing here? Selling something?

GUY. I'm actually on a break from all that. Needed to get away from that world.

JOLEY 14. So you came here?

GUY. What's wrong with here?

JOLEY 14. Are you kidding?

GUY. It seems like a very pleasant place with nice people. Clean. Safe.

JOLEY 14. Things aren't always what they seem.

GUY. Oh, so please. Fill me in on my new, but temporary place of residence.

JOLEY 14. Just what I said. Nothing's as peaceful as it sounds.

GUY. Nothing.

JOLEY 14. You were out in the fields, but you heard crickets. I was sitting on these porch steps, but then I heard your whistle. And now . . .

GUY. I've broken your silence.

JOLEY 14. Not you.

GUY. Who then?

Joley 14 can't answer. She rises, walks down the porch steps, away from Guy, downstage, and looks out on to the field. Joley 30 emerges and stands beside Joley 14. The lights go down on Joley 14 but remain on Joley 30. The present.

JOLEY 30. When I was six, this guy came to live with my mother and me. He was her "friend" and his name was Bo. I know. Sounds funny now. But that's one of the reasons she got together with him. Because of that name. My mother thought "Bo" sounded like something out of *Gone With The Wind*, so she had to have this Bo. I had never known my real father, not that I cared, but she did. Ma thought I needed that "father figure" in my life. The truth was, she needed it more. I can honestly say that my mother was the neediest person I had ever known. She needed attention, and approval, constant approval, and love, or at least knowing . . . or listening to someone tell her he loved her. And that's what this Bo gave her. But it was cool, at first. I didn't really notice him very much. He worked days, come home, and pass out. Bo sold used cars down on the highway. He made good money. Until he was fired for coming to work too late, being rude to potential customers, and drinking beer in the front seat of the Oldsmobile in the dealership's lot. I thought she would throw his lazy ass out for screwing up like that. But she couldn't. She felt sorry for him. So she got this job, working nights, in this coffee shop off the highway. This was before she did hair. I remember the first night she went to work. I didn't want her to go. I didn't understand why, but I had this thing . . . force seeping through me. Overpowering me. It was like something bad . . . terrible would happen. And I couldn't speak. I couldn't move. I felt . . . bad. It was the kind of bad that crawls up into your throat. It paralyzes you. Until you're just standing there, and you become . . . nothing. Perhaps that inability to communicate protects you in a twisted way. Or at least it gives you the notion you're being protected. It hides what's happening. Maybe at that time you're unable to see or hear or speak about what's really going on. Because it's the bad that's so terrible, you can't even say it out loud, because you're afraid once it's said it'll happen.

The past. The light leaves Joley 30 and returns to Joley 14.

GUY. If you could be anywhere in the world, doing anything at this time, what would it be?

JOLEY 14. I don't know.

GUY (*playfully*). Come on!

JOLEY 14. I honestly don't know.

GUY. Come on, Joley. What would you do? Where would you be?

JOLEY 14. I'd be driving. Driving down the highway, all through the night. And out of this place.

Guy stands behind Joley 14 as the two look at the field.

GUY. Where to?

JOLEY 14. It wouldn't matter. I'd just drive.

GUY. Why?

JOLEY 14. Because it would be the most free thing anyone could do. Going through the night, stopping as little as possible. Looking at the empty road ahead of you. Knowing it belongs to you, only you, completely. Looking up at the sky. Looking at the colors of the night. Feeling the night air. Listening to it. Watching everyone as they're asleep. Knowing more than they do, because you've been awake and they've been asleep. So you have a point over them. It's like they missed something that you didn't.

GUY. Sounds like an attractive plan.

JOLEY 14. You asked.

GUY. What would you do when the road ended?

JOLEY 14. It wouldn't.

GUY (*laughing*). It has to sometime. Everything else does.

JOLEY 14. It wouldn't matter. I'd be far from here. That's the only thing that matters.

GUY. Why don't you do it?

JOLEY 14. What?

GUY. Leave. Tonight.

JOLEY 14. Can't.

GUY. What's stopping you?

JOLEY 14. No license. No car.

GUY. Sounds like an excuse. Get someone else to go with you. I know you wouldn't have any problem finding some sixteen-year-old male willing to take a road trip with you.

JOLEY 14. It wouldn't be the same.

GUY. Why?

JOLEY 14. Someone else's roof—someone else's rules.

GUY. It doesn't have to be that way.

JOLEY 14. Doesn't it?

GUY (*looking outward*). What do you see?

JOLEY 14. The same thing you do.

GUY. I don't think so.

JOLEY 14. Mosquitoes, buzzing around. Fireflies popping in and outta sight with their orange color. Tall grass that's dead and needs to be cut. The breeze, making it wave back and forth a little. Things. Night things. But really, it's just . . . big, wide, open endless space. Nothing.

GUY. It doesn't lead to anything?

JOLEY 14. It's not supposed to.

GUY. Why can't it?

JOLEY 14. If it did, I'd never want to leave.

GUY. Why do you want to leave?

JOLEY 14. I have to.

GUY. Your ma wants you out?

JOLEY 14. That's not why.

GUY. Tell me, then.

JOLEY 14. I'm afraid.

GUY. Of what?

JOLEY 14. Of staying.

GUY. But everything out there . . . fireflies and tall grass . . . everything looks so . . . peaceful.

JOLEY 14. That's what it wants you to think.

GUY. But what do you think is really out there?

JOLEY 14. Noise. A lot of noise.

GUY. Why don't you close it out?

JOLEY 14. I can't.

GUY. Shut your eyes and close out the noise.

JOLEY 14. Why do you care?

GUY. You need someone to, Joley. That's all. I mean no harm. Believe that. I could tell, from the school, that you were different, unique. You need someone. I'd like it to be me. I want you to know that I can protect you.

JOLEY 14. What makes you think I need protection?

GUY. You've been saying it from the moment we met. Perhaps you didn't realize it, but that's what you've been calling out for.

JOLEY 14. Who are you?

GUY. Your friend. (*Joley 14 turns to Guy. She's unsure, but leans closer to him. She closes her eyes, and continues to lean into him. Guy responds by kissing her on the forehead. Joley 14 is surprised, but relieved.*) Go inside now. Into your house. Up your stairs. To your room. And to sleep.

JOLEY 14. I can't.

GUY. You have to.

JOLEY 14. Why can't I stay here?

GUY. It's time to go. You know you have to.

JOLEY 14. You won't get into any trouble. I'll make sure of that.

GUY. That's real good to know, Joley, but it's late.

JOLEY 14. You're not leaving town yet, are you?

GUY. Not yet.

JOLEY 14. You'll tell me before you go?

GUY. Of course. So, it looks like you won't mind talking to me again.

JOLEY 14. I won't mind.

GUY. I'm glad.

JOLEY 14. And I won't tell anyone about you.

GUY. But Joley, what's there to tell?

JOLEY 14. Nothing, I guess.

GUY. That's right. Nothing to speak about. So go inside and to
sleep.

*Joley 14 slowly walks up the porch steps. She opens the screen door,
enters the house, and watches Guy from behind the door. Lights go
down on Joley 14 and Guy. Guy remains at the fence, looking onto
the field. He begins to whistle a tranquil tune. The light goes back
to Joley 18 and Stone on the dark roadside.*

JOLEY 18. It's too quiet.

STONE. It's too loud with those damn crickets.

JOLEY 18. I wish I could just . . . sleep off this quiet.

STONE. Still having trouble?

JOLEY 18. Yeah.

STONE. Need some help?

JOLEY 18. Not now.

STONE. Your call. It's here for the asking. (*Turns away.*)

JOLEY 18. Are you sorry I'm here?

STONE. Stop it.

JOLEY 18. What?

STONE. Looking for reassurance from me.

JOLEY 18. I wasn't.

STONE. You were. You do. It gets tiring. When I get bored with this,
you'll know. Believe me.

JOLEY 18. I hope so, because I don't like wasting my time.

STONE. Is that what you think you're doing with me?

JOLEY 18. I don't know.

STONE. No, you don't. First you tell me, and we agreed, to keep
things cool. No questions. No commitment. Nothing. Next

thing you tell me you love me and you get pissed if I don't say it back!

JOLEY 18. So what if I do? What's the big deal? Don't worry. It's just words, right? No meaning attached. Promise.

STONE. You're too much. (*Rolls over to sleep. Joley 14 looks over him.*)

JOLEY 18. And you're too little.

Lights down on Joley 18 and Stone.

The past. Lights up on Joley 14. It is day, and she is re-wiring the fence. We hear whistles from offstage, like catcalls. Ray and Jo-Jo, each carrying a beer, run up to Joley 14.

RAY. Whatcha doin Joley?

JOLEY 14. What's it look like?

JO-JO. Like you're cutting your dainty little hands to ribbons trying to fix your tired old fence.

RAY. And getting heatstroke at the same time doin' it.

JO-JO. Not even noon and it's already reached the triple digits. Did you know that, Joley? One hundred degrees! All I can say is glad I don't have to do hard labor in this heat.

RAY. Couldn't find some poor sap to do it for you?

JO-JO. Bet she could, though. Couldn't you, Joley? I bet you wouldn't find no trouble at all getting someone to help you out.

RAY. So quiet. Just like at school.

JO-JO. Damn depressing.

RAY. I'll say.

JOLEY 14. Why don't you two just get going.

JO-JO. Nah. We're having too much fun chatting away with you, girl.

RAY. My God! She looks like she's gonna melt right under the sun. Here, Joley, a peace offering. (*Holds out the beer. Joley 14 takes a long sip and hands it back, wiping her mouth with the back of her hand.*) See. We ain't so bad. Just tryin' to be friendly.

JO-JO. You check out the graduation?

JOLEY 14. I was busy.

RAY. Missed a fuckin' great party! We're finally outta that prison.

JOLEY 14. Some of us aren't so lucky.

JO-JO. But I bet you like school. You seem like the smart type. You know, that dark, quiet, deep-thinkin' type. Are you, Joley?

Joley 14 takes Ray's beer back for another sip.

JOLEY 14. Whatever you think.

RAY. Where's your ma?

JO-JO. Damn fine-lookin' woman.

JOLEY 14. Out.

JO-JO. Anybody home?

JOLEY 14. No.

RAY. Got no old man around?

JO-JO. Which one?

JOLEY 14. What do you know?

JO-JO. Like mother like daughter.

JOLEY 14. Like no one!

JO-JO. That's not what I hear.

JOLEY 14. What do you hear?

RAY. Why you got no friends, Joley?

JO-JO. Aw, come on. Our girl's too sophisticated for our little town.

JOLEY 14. Yeah, right.

RAY. She just don't fit. Girlfriend thinks she's too good for us.

JOLEY 14. Yeah, right. I'm too good for everyone! Look where I live! Look what I'm doing! We're more alike than you think. Unfortunately.

JO-JO (*to Ray*). See, that's what you don't get with the other girls. Real talk, you know. And that's what our little Joley gives us.

RAY. One of the things.

JOLEY 14. You two can't find anyone else to latch onto today?

RAY. Now why should we go and find someone else, when we've got you.

JO-JO. The silent type works best.

Joley 14 puts the wire down, and attempts to move away. Ray and Jo-Jo block her path.

RAY. We're not finished yet.

JO-JO. Hell, no! We just got here!

JOLEY 14. Outta my way!

RAY. We're here to find out.

JOLEY 14. What?

JO-JO. Whether what they all say is true.

JOLEY 14. About what?

RAY. You, of course.

JOLEY 14. What do they say?

JO-JO. Always thought you to be the type not to care what others said.

JOLEY 14. There's nothing to say.

RAY. That's not what we heard!

JOLEY 14. From whom?

JO-JO (*mockingly*). Whom? People!

RAY. Guys.

JOLEY 14. What guys?

JO-JO. Secret.

RAY. Nah, we can tell. The ones your ma's been with.

JOLEY 14. You're a liar!

JO-JO. You like to share, eh?

JOLEY 14. Who said this?

RAY. Too many to name.

JOLEY 14. You're full of shit!

JO-JO. See, it's always the ones like Joley who give you the best and biggest surprises.

RAY. And she's been keeping her secrets for a long time.

JO-JO. We just wanted to find out for ourselves.

JOLEY 14. There's nothing to find out!

JO-JO. Now that's not true! That's not true at all. You do care about what others think. That's why you're getting so upset with your two new best friends.

RAY. Can't escape it. (*To Jo-Jo*) Look at her eyes. All big, dark, and wide.

JO-JO. I see.

JOLEY 14 (*turning away*). Nothing to see.

RAY (*turning her around*). Sure there is. Those deep eyes can tell us a lot of stories. They tell us "this girl's been around." But she's good. She knows how to stay quiet.

JO-JO. I wonder who she's been protecting all these years.

RAY. I bet an older guy.

JOLEY 14. I can shout! Louder than anyone! And I wouldn't care who heard!

JO-JO. But no one's listening, Joley.

RAY (*pulling her to overlook the swamp*). Look where we are. We're nowhere.

JO-JO. Just the three of us!

RAY. And damn, I wanna be one of the stories your eyes tell.

JO-JO. Me too.

JOLEY 14. You can't tell anything from looking at me! Stop playing like you do!

RAY. But we can. That's why we're here.

JO-JO. We always could, girl. We just had to wait for the right time to tell you. That's all.

RAY. And we've just been told a hell of a lot, just now. Just by looking at you.

JO-JO. So don't disappoint us after we've come so far. (*He and Ray grab Joley 14 who in turn grabs a long sharp wire from the fence with which she slashes Jo-Jo across his face, and tears Ray's shirt).* Crazy fucking bitch! (*He lies on the ground, bleeding.*)

Ray lunges at Joley 14. Joley 14 fights Ray, but silently. She's having difficulty breathing.

JOLEY 14 (*whispering*). I can shout! I swear to you! People'll come running through that field.

RAY. Go ahead. (*Joley 14 is trying to scream, but no shout leaves her lips.*) Where's it then? Where is your big loud shout to the heavens? Where is it Joley? Come on! Let's be heard!

A sharp piercing whistle is heard. Ray stops. Enter Guy.

GUY (*low*). Get off her.

RAY. Fuck off!

With tremendous strength Guy pulls a shocked Ray off Joley 14. Guy throws Ray to the ground next to Jo-Jo, takes some wire from the fence, and holds it at Ray's jugular.

GUY. Now run. Before I kill you both.

JO-JO. Psycho bitch started it! She was beggin' for it. From both of us! You shoulda seen her! And that's what everyone in this shit town is gonna hear!

RAY. Good people oughtta know they gotta whore livin' here!

JO-JO. Your secret's out, girl! (*Runs off with Ray.*)

Joley 14 remains on the ground. Guy looks at his hands, bloody from the wire. Then throws the wire to the ground. Joley 14 stays sitting, looking down. Guy takes a handkerchief from his immaculately white jacket and wipes his hands. He then extends his now-clean hand to Joley 14.

GUY. Take my hand. (*Joley 14 doesn't move. He continues, gently*) Please.

Joley 14 looks up at Guy, then at his extended hand. Slowly, carefully, she puts her hand in his. Then slowly gets up. Guy, gently, like a parent, takes off his jacket and places it around her. She puts her hands around her throat.

JOLEY 14. Nothing would come out.

GUY. Don't worry. They're gone now. They won't bother you again. They're just little boys.

JOLEY 14 (*still in shock*). I told them I could scream. Louder than anyone or anything.

GUY. Joley, they're gone. I'm here. Your friend's here.

JOLEY 14. Why wouldn't any sound come out? (*Upset.*) Why not? (*Self-assuring.*) I was screaming. Inside. So loud! Louder than anything else in this whole world, but it wouldn't leave me. It wouldn't leave my guts. It was buried deep, inside. But it couldn't go any further. It couldn't go up, through my lungs, into my throat and out my mouth! It was silenced. I silenced it. But I could feel the sounds and the words on my lips. That was it. The scream was only for me. Not for Jo-Jo or Ray or anyone else. But it wasn't for me. I wanted to be heard . . . but . . . it was like there was some force that wouldn't let me be heard. Why wouldn't it let me?

GUY. It was fear. That's all. A large dose of plain old fear.

JOLEY 14 (*adamantly*). It was more than that.

GUY. Doesn't matter now.

JOLEY 14. It does. Something prevented me from being heard. But I remember some sound . . . like a wild animal. It made some piercing sound, that made him stop.

GUY. There was no animal.

JOLEY 14. I'm sure it was. I remember that. And then you came.

GUY. Joley, that was me! Remember? That was my whistle.

JOLEY 14 (*shocked*). You? It couldn't have been.

GUY. Why?

JOLEY 14. It couldn't have come from a human. Not a real human person. It didn't sound like one. I would've thought maybe a wild bird . . . or black crow . . . something else . . .

GUY (*taking Joley 14 by the arm*). Look at me! And see me, Joley. I saved you.

JOLEY 14 (*quietly and fearfully*). Thank you. (*Pulls away.*)

GUY. You look at me differently, and I don't understand why.

JOLEY 14 (*turning away*). I don't.

GUY. Don't lie to me.

JOLEY 14. What made you come here today?

GUY. I told you I'd be back

JOLEY 14. What brought you here, now? At this moment? You could've picked any other moment in the whole entire day! Why this one?

GUY. I don't know what you want to hear, Joley.

JOLEY 14. Who are you?

GUY. I've told you.

JOLEY 14. You're just a guy.

GUY. Is that all to you?

JOLEY 14. Not really.

GUY. You're upset. That's all. And rightfully so. You can't know what you're saying.

JOLEY 14. Maybe not. They'll come back.

GUY. Nah. They'll stay away for a long time.

JOLEY 14. They meant what they said. They'll do it too. Tell tales. Go around and tell anyone who'll listen, and that's everyone around here! Cause that's all they do in this place! Listen to filthy lies and gossip! These people here'll listen to trash like Ray and Jo-Jo way before they'll listen to me! My mother would believe them before she would believe me.

GUY. You're wrong. I know their kind. Those boys'll do nothing. Cowards! The both of them! Biggest ones imaginable.

JOLEY 14. How do you know?

GUY (*defensively*). You meet lots of types along the way. Those two are just another addition to the collection of people you come across. I've seen them before. Different names and faces, of course, but let's just say, those two are unfortunately very familiar.

JOLEY 14. Am I another addition to your collection too?

GUY. Of course not.

JOLEY 14. Why not? What makes me so different?

GUY. You best go inside and clean yourself up before your ma gets back.

JOLEY 14. Ray played football for the school team. Co-captain. He's never lost a fight. And he's been in plenty, especially after he's been drinking. You sure don't look like you could beat him in a fight. I can't really picture everything again, but he didn't know what hit him when you came along.

GUY. Just inner strength, Joley.

JOLEY 14. I think that was the first time anyone ever scared him.

GUY. You have that same strength.

JOLEY 14. No, I don't. I couldn't even speak.

GUY. It's there. But you haven't found it yet. Go home now. Put all this away.

Guy approaches Joley 14 and kisses her on the forehead. She is shaken, but doesn't reject him. Joley 14 slowly backs toward the house. Guy watches her. The lights fade on Guy but remain on Joley 14, standing on the porch, still wearing Guy's jacket. She is still shaken and stares fixedly at the field. The lights stay on Joley 14 but also go up on Joley 30 who speaks to the audience.

JOLEY 30. My mother went through this spiritual call, or something like that, for a few years. It was after Bo split, and though she never said anything, I think she knew. About Bo and me, and what had happened, and what she didn't say, and what she didn't see, or didn't want to see. I think that's why she liked being away so much. She wouldn't have to see anything. It wouldn't be by choice, but by pure absence. She wouldn't be called on it. It was something unavoidable. Afterwards, she spoke to me, without saying anything. There were words, but nothing was said. It was like, a code which started after Bo left, and continued for years. Everything was said in halves, like a comedy routine. Someone would start, and divulge very little information, while the other partner had to guess what to think and react and say next. It could be a very useful skill finishing someone else's sentences, answering the question before it's even asked, knowing what someone's thinking. But sometimes it's better or easier not to know. So to ease her guilt, without a voice, she found God. Actually she found this church in town with a lot of good-looking men, eligible and ineligible. So we went. And she tried. She thought she was doing good. Bringing something good or something that had the appearance of good to both of us. And she wanted so badly to be like them, the Rays and Jo-Jos and . . . guys . . . and everyone else who fit that description. Pure and clean and white, good, from the outside, of course. But it was pretty, and different, different from what she had experienced. So she embraced it. The building was sterile. Everything was still, and old and quiet. She equated goodness with quiet . . . silence. That's how she measured my behavior every Sunday. If I were quiet and still, I was acceptable for her and for them. You can almost lose your voice, when it hasn't been used for so long. You discipline yourself not to. And you never learn to shout, even when you need to. I didn't learn to shout for a long time after that. I kept silent. Unintentionally. I was unable to do anything else. I heard shouts. And words. And whistles. And then, later on, I learned to do it myself. I spoke.

Stone awakens to the sound of a piercing whistle. Joley 18 is unaffected by the sound.

STONE. You hear something?

JOLEY 18. Like what?

STONE. I don't know. Something strange.

JOLEY 18. Now you're afraid?

STONE. Hell no! It was just . . . real weird. You didn't hear it?

JOLEY 18. I don't know. Maybe. Was it an animal?

STONE. Think so. Hope so. It was a piercing sound. Kinda painful, you know. Like a cry.

JOLEY 18. There was nothing.

STONE. You seem real sure of yourself.

JOLEY 18. About some things.

STONE. Only some?

JOLEY 18. You know that.

STONE. Yeah, I do. Too bad.

JOLEY 18. Yeah, too bad.

Stone goes back to sleep. Joley 18 rises and looks out toward the field. She and Joley 14 look in the same direction. The lights slowly fade on Stone and Joley 18 and return completely to Joley 14, who is standing on the porch wearing Guy's jacket. She feels an unease and takes the jacket off and throws it to the ground. Enter Lily from the field, holding a fistful of wire.

LILY. And what's this wire doing all over the place? You left the fence half-done and this garbage all over the field!

Beat.

JOLEY 14 (*reflectively*). It got too hot to work.

LILY. So you leave it for me to clean up?

JOLEY 14 (*hesitantly*). I was going to do it.

LILY. When?

JOLEY 14. When it got cooler.

LILY. And if someone got hurt?

JOLEY 14 (*quietly*). Someone already has.

LILY. What?

JOLEY 14. Then he'll bleed, right?

LILY. What's gotten into you? (*Notices Joley 14's torn clothes and dishevelled appearance.*) What happened?

JOLEY 14. I fell into the wiring.

LILY. Well, you best change and put something on those cuts.

JOLEY 14 (*hesitantly*). Okay.

LILY. You want to tell me something?

JOLEY 14. No.

LILY. I'm tired of fighting, Joley.

JOLEY 14. Me too.

LILY. I wish I could believe you.

JOLEY 14. You never did.

LILY. What do you mean?

JOLEY 14. Nothing.

LILY. What are you waiting for? I told you to get cleaned up.

JOLEY 14. That wouldn't help.

LILY. If you have something to say, say it!

JOLEY 14. Don't you care?

LILY. Oh, for God's sake! Is this gonna be about how I never did enough for you, cared enough for you? Because if it is . . . I'm not in the mood to listen to your attacking me today!

JOLEY 14. Not what I think, but what they think.

LILY. Who?

JOLEY 14. Everyone. You know . . . you . . . me . . . us . . . that's it! Just us. Not one man, but too many men.

LILY. What the hell have you been up to?

JOLEY 14. Nothing! Absolutely nothing! But they . . . Ms. Hanley, and Ray and Jo-Jo and the church choir and the reverend and the church deacons and the town . . . they wouldn't care! They would still have their minds made up! You know that! Don't you care? Doesn't that anger you?

LILY. You're angering me now, because I don't know what in the hell you're talking about!

JOLEY 14. Yeah, you do. We're not them. Why can't you see that?

LILY. See? You want me to see things? And listen? To what others are saying? You think I have the time you have to do that?

JOLEY 14. Why stay?

LILY. Why stay? You wanna leave, Joley? You know where the door is, don't you? If this isn't good enough, please, feel free to leave!

JOLEY 14. I'm not asking for me, but you!

LILY. Why? You care what they say about your ma?

JOLEY 14. Yeah! I do!

LILY. Why?

JOLEY 14. I have to.

LILY. You don't have to do anything. There. I said it. You have my permission, to go on, then. (*Approaches Joley 14, who remains still.*) That's right. You've learned earlier than I did, lucky girl. You've answered your own question. (*Touches Joley 14's arm.*) Cold. That's how I feel. You've just learned what took me too long to figure out. Your feet are frozen in the mud. You're stuck. See? Stuck people don't leave, because they can't. Go? Go where? To who? Who's waiting, Joley? Your dad? Where's he? I don't know. We wonder. I still do. Does he? How can he not? How does someone do that, Joley? Walk away. But he wasn't stuck, you see. So he could.

JOLEY 14 (*quietly*). Did I make you "stuck?"

LILY. No. Me, maybe you, I don't really know, but me, and people like me, are put on this earth, with no place to go.

JOLEY 14. And me? Will I have a place to go?

LILY. I don't know.

JOLEY 14. You're supposed to.

LILY. Says who?

JOLEY 14. You're supposed . . .

LILY (*interrupting*). To be more? To . . . give you this . . . safe place? Is that what I'm supposed to do?

JOLEY 14. Yes.

LILY. I know of no such place, so I can't give you one.

JOLEY 14. I can't believe you just said that.

LILY. At least I'm honest.

JOLEY 14. I don't like being us.

LILY (*laughs off*). Could be worse, right?

JOLEY 14 (*softly*). Right.

LILY. So why don't we just go on, then? Get cleaned up, and remember, no more mess on the field.

JOLEY 14. I'll try to keep clean.

LILY. You do that.

Joley 14 doesn't move. Lily acknowledges Joley 14's silent protest. Lily ignores Joley 14 and enters the house. Joley 14 is left on the porch, looking out at the swamp. Lights down.

Lights up on Joley 14. Same day, late night. The stage is dark, like the night. A light is on Joley 14, sitting in a rocking chair on the porch in her bathrobe. Someone whistles a sweet-sounding tune. Joley 14 sits up in fear, but remains in her chair.

JOLEY 14 (*quietly*). Guy?

Guy makes himself seen and approaches the porch, still wearing his immaculately white suit but without the jacket.

GUY. Know anyone else who can whistle like that?

Joley 14 hands Guy his jacket.

JOLEY 14. Here. I ironed it for you.

GUY. You didn't have to do that.

JOLEY 14. I can see you take real good care of your clothes.

GUY. Appearances are important. After all, they do give the first impression.

JOLEY 14. Well, thanks for letting me borrow it.

GUY. Any visitors tonight?

JOLEY 14. No.

GUY. Told you! You've gotta learn to trust me a little more. Those boys won't be back.

JOLEY 14. What were you doing out there?

GUY. Just taking a walk. Air's cooled down a bit. And since we've got a bit of relief, thought I may take advantage of it. What were you doing?

JOLEY 14. Just thinking.

GUY. About what?

JOLEY 14. About driving far away.

GUY. Sounds tempting.

JOLEY 14. Tonight would've been the perfect night to go.

GUY. Why tonight?

JOLEY 14. Like you said. Air's cool. A bit of relief from the heat . . .

GUY. And your ma's not home. So there'd be no one to stop you.

JOLEY 14. She wouldn't stop me. She'd probably help me pack.

GUY. Now I can't believe that. I may not know your relationship with your ma too well, but what I do know is that parents love their kids! Especially mas. And that's the bottom line. Despite all the arguments you two may have. She loves you, and that's the truth!

JOLEY 14. What about you, Guy?

GUY. What about me?

JOLEY 14. You seem to have a strong opinion on families. Do you have one?

GUY. Doesn't everyone?

JOLEY 14. I don't know. I don't know everyone.

GUY (*chuckling*). Smart mouth for everything, don't you? Well I did. Once.

JOLEY 14. What happened?

GUY. Now, Joley. I don't think we should go there.

JOLEY 14. Why not? You sure know a lot about me. I think friendship . . . trust . . . needs to be fair, you know? No secrets. That's when things get bad. When people keep secrets from each other.

GUY. Perhaps when you get older, you'll realize that there are some things that are better kept secret.

JOLEY 14 (*angrily*). Don't give me that older shit! I am old! I know . . . things! Things I wish I didn't know, but were told to me in ways that would give the "older" adults thoughts of terrible things dancing in their heads at night! There'll be nothing for me to realize when I'm "older." There's nothing new for me to learn.

Beat.

GUY. I'm sorry. I shouldn't have spoken down to you like that. I should've known better.

JOLEY 14. You should've.

GUY. And yes, I do think that you may know more than those silly kids at that school of yours.

JOLEY 14. Most definitely.

GUY. I truly am sorry, Joley, for doubting you. Forgive me.

JOLEY 14. I just want to know.

GUY. Why?

JOLEY 14. Because of what happened today. Because of what you did for me.

GUY. It was nothing.

JOLEY 14. It was a lot. There's so much anger inside of me, but I can't let it out. That's why I was silent. I'm afraid of releasing all the anger and the noise, but I don't know when it'll happen, or where it'll go! I'm afraid of myself. Of . . .

GUY. Losing control.

JOLEY 14. That's right. Has that ever happened to you? Is that why you're alone now, Guy?

Beat.

GUY. Manipulative little one, aren't you?

JOLEY 14 (*shocked*). What?

GUY. Twisting things! Using yourself to get your answers! Trying to trick me into telling you! That's not good, Joley, that's not good at all!

JOLEY 14. I was talking about myself! I wasn't tricking you! I wasn't even thinking of doing that!

GUY. I thought you were different, from the others. They're all so silly and foolish, but you looked so pained, and true! You looked like you could understand.

JOLEY 14. I'm not at all like these people! I think I'm more like you. That's why I want to know who you are.

GUY. Oh, Joley. You're not like me. Not at all.

JOLEY 14. You don't know that.

GUY. I do.

JOLEY 14. What's different?

GUY. Those boys. Those little boys you were with, with their cans of beer and stupid jokes and little boy voices and laughter! Do you hate them, Joley?

JOLEY 14. Of course I do.

GUY. How much?

JOLEY 14. I don't know. A lot. You can't measure hate. All of it's bad.

GUY. Do you hate them enough to harm them?

JOLEY 14. Maybe.

GUY. You don't!

JOLEY 14. I could!

GUY. No, Joley. Don't lie to yourself. Don't be pretending to be someone you are not.

JOLEY 14. Who do you think I am?

GUY. A girl. A young woman. Who hasn't lost control.

JOLEY 14. Yet.

GUY. If it hasn't happened now, it's not going to.

JOLEY 14. Has it happened to you? (*Beat. Guy looks at his hands. She persists.*) Because you could tell me. I'd understand. Guy! I'm afraid you have this image of me that just isn't so. I could listen to you. I want to.

GUY. It's these people!

JOLEY 14. I know.

GUY. You don't! They do it to you. Don't you see? They're the ones who make you act! And shout! People like those boys of yours! And even people like you.

JOLEY 14. I haven't done anything to harm you.

GUY. You're just like them.

JOLEY 14. Stop saying that! I'm not!

GUY. In a different way. But you also, make me act, and shout . . .

JOLEY 14 (*realizing*). And whistle.

GUY. I wanted to kill them. And protect you.

JOLEY 14. That's you. Not me!

GUY. And you.

JOLEY 14. No! We do things that we want to do! Don't go pinning your actions on other people! Damn! I hate that! Why can't people take responsibility for their own doing! They are so afraid; it makes me sick! And then they go on blaming others for all the bad that's happened! No one wants to take responsibility! Especially adults!

GUY. You're so quick to speak, aren't you? Oh yes, the big, bad grown-ups are the ones acting like the children. Why don't you lead the way? Oh, Joley, you can honestly say that every single little thing you've done in your life has been by choice? Think, Joley! Do you mean to tell me that no one has ever forced you to do anything that you didn't want to do? Ever?

Beat.

JOLEY 14. It isn't the same.

GUY. Oh, it is.

JOLEY 14. No! Because I have never hurt anyone.

GUY. Except yourself.

JOLEY 14. What has someone made you do?

GUY. It's difficult, you know. There are some people out there, who evoke very deep and strong feelings, and you fight them, honestly, you try, but . . . they win. And you lose.

JOLEY 14. Your control.

GUY. That's right. It isn't many people, just perhaps one or two out there who've stirred such overwhelming thoughts. They're so overwhelming, that it's like you're someone else, and you can't get yourself back until you've done something to alleviate those feelings.

JOLEY 14. So you do evil?

GUY. What is evil anyway?

JOLEY 14. You shouldn't have to ask. You just know.

GUY. So killing is evil?

JOLEY 14. Yes.

GUY. In every case?

JOLEY 14. Yes.

GUY. What about self-defense?

JOLEY 14. I guess that'd be different.

GUY. So that wouldn't be evil?

JOLEY 14. No.

GUY. So it isn't wrong in every case!

JOLEY 14. No. I don't know! Why? Have you ever killed anyone? (*Guy is silent and turns away from Joley 14.*) Have you?

A breeze blows by. Guy looks out at the field. Joley 14 has her answer. She is fearful, and steps away from Guy.

GUY (*still looking away from Joley 14, onto the swamp*). You're looking at me differently now.

JOLEY 14. No.

GUY. You are. I feel your fear.

JOLEY 14. Should I be afraid?

GUY. What do you think?

JOLEY 14. I don't know.

GUY. I could tell you anything. Your words, Joley.

JOLEY 14. You can.

GUY. Not anymore.

JOLEY 14 (*searchingly*). Was it . . . self-defense? Or someone made you do it, right? I mean, like a fight? Or an accident? That's OK. Things happen, right. I know. I mean, I haven't ever killed anyone, but I think I know the feeling afterward. You don't expect it, but, all of a sudden you've found yourself in a strange place, and you don't know how you got there. Is that what happened?

GUY. You could've killed those boys today.

JOLEY 14. No.

GUY. But you struck them.

JOLEY 14. I know I wouldn't have been able to do more.

GUY. Something stopped you?

JOLEY 14. Yes.

GUY. Me?

JOLEY 14. No. Something else.

GUY. Something inside you.

JOLEY 14. Yes. But I don't know exactly what it was.

GUY. But it's there. Like a censor. It stops you from being in a place you don't belong.

JOLEY 14. Yeah. That's what it feels like. Something's watching me. Stopping me from . . .

GUY. Losing control.

JOLEY 14. But I don't like it all the time.

GUY. Why? What else does it do?

JOLEY 14. It won't let me be heard! It won't let me shout!

GUY. That's when it's bad. It's as if you have to have both. Its good uses and its bad uses.

JOLEY 14. Were you ever stopped? Is there a warning inside you? Telling you, it's too far, go back before it's too late?

GUY. No.

JOLEY 14. I'm sorry.

GUY. Why?

JOLEY 14. Because it isn't fair.

GUY. I don't mind. I'd rather be heard than be silenced. I think that's the worst thing in the world—silence.

A light remains on Joley 14 and Guy, but Joley 30, on the other side of the stage, now commands our attention. The present.

JOLEY 30 (*to audience*). In every house, there's a secret room, or wardrobe, or desk drawer clearly marked "do not enter." But we ignore all the warnings and turn that knob, and peer inside, and enter that small, dark world that place has to offer. The first time is a thrill. An exhilarating ride! But no one's there to bear witness to our conquest of defying all reprimands. So we enter again and again. But not for the excitement, not anymore. It all wore off after the first or second time. We know we shouldn't be there, but we go back, because it reminds us of something. We know it. No surprises. It becomes familiar territory. It's waiting for us. No pretense. No expectations. It's home. Even if that home is heat and darkness and flies and swamp and Rays and Jo-Jos and waist-high spiked-wire fences that cut your fingers and . . . whistles. We know it. Despite that gnawing inside telling us to get out. Hurry up and leave this place before something very bad happens. But we don't. Why should we? What would happen next? So we keep coming back, until it becomes a part of us.

The light stays on Joley 30, but also travels to the roadside to Joley 18 and a sleeping Stone. Joley 18 is propped against Stone's car and looking up at the sky. Joley 30 stands next to the roadside couple and speaks to Joley 18.

JOLEY 30. What's going on?

JOLEY 18. Nothing much.

JOLEY 30. Headed up North?

JOLEY 18. Don't know.

JOLEY 30. So you're just driving.

JOLEY 18. Looks like it.

JOLEY 30. It's the right night for a drive to nowhere.

JOLEY 18. That's why we're here.

Beat.

JOLEY 30. *(referring to Stone)*. Poor boy.

JOLEY 18. You pity him?

JOLEY 30. Shall I pity you?

JOLEY 18. You don't need to pity any of us.

JOLEY 30. He thinks it's about him.

JOLEY 18. "It?" "It" what?

JOLEY 30. This . . . this place . . . you two. He thinks it's all him.

JOLEY 18. It is.

JOLEY 30. Is it?

Beat.

JOLEY 18. Why don't you turn around and head back where you came from!

JOLEY 30. Ma was wrong.

JOLEY 18. She's got nothing to do with this!

JOLEY 30. You've already won, but you don't see it. You're not stuck. There is a place for you.

JOLEY 18. No, there isn't.

JOLEY 30. Why deny yourself?

JOLEY 18. It's truth. Not everyone is born with a place to go.

JOLEY 30. You're right. But you're not one of them. But Ma was.

JOLEY 18. I've accepted where I am.

JOLEY 30. Where are you? How can you accept what isn't even finished yet?

JOLEY 18. There's no progression. So I went a few states away! Big shit! We're still stuck. She was right.

JOLEY 30. She was wrong. Let it go.

JOLEY 18. There you go again with this "it!" I'm not holding anything, so there's no "it" for me to let go!

JOLEY 30 *(referring to Stone)*. Let him in.

JOLEY 18. He doesn't deserve it.

JOLEY 30. But you do.

The past. Guy silences Joley 30 and Joley 18. Lights go down on the roadside and focus again on Guy and Joley 14. The past. The same night on the porch.

GUY. Shhh! Listen!

JOLEY 14. I didn't hear anything.

GUY. You're not listening hard enough.

JOLEY 14. It's so still.

GUY. That's what night sounds like. After it's been stripped bare of all light and people and work, until it becomes this . . . absolute stillness. (*Joley 14 stays silent and looks out at the swamp.*) I'll stay away. If that's what you want. (*Joley 14 stays silent.*) I never wanted to cause you any distress. That was never my intention, Joley. I hope you can believe that. I just wanted to be your friend, and keep you safe. That was all. But if you can't help but look at me differently, if you don't want my friendship, I'll stay outside that fence. I'll stay further than outside that fence. I'll keep out. But only if that's what you want.

JOLEY 14. It's nice having someone . . . who's there . . . watching. It's safe, you know. Knowing someone's . . . just there for you.

GUY. I bet you never had that before. Have you, Joley? Has anyone been keeping watch?

JOLEY 14 (*painfully*). No.

GUY. I didn't think so. That's why I'm here.

JOLEY 14. I know.

GUY. Shall I go?

JOLEY 14 (*quietly*). No.

GUY. I just want to do what's right, by keeping you safe.

JOLEY 14. Thank you. (*Moves closer to Guy.*)

Guy kisses her gently on the lips. Joley 14 remains very still.

GUY. I'll be thinking of you tonight.

JOLEY 14. You'll stay around?

GUY. If that's what you want.

JOLEY 14. It is.

Guy steps off her porch.

GUY. Sleep, Joley.

JOLEY 14. Come back.

GUY (*soothingly*). I will. (*He leaves.*)

Joley 14 remains on the porch. The lights go down on her and up on the other side of the stage to Joley 18 and Stone. Joley 18 stands away from the parked car and camped-out Stone, who is now awake.

STONE. What time is it?

JOLEY 18. Late.

STONE. Come over here.

Joley 18 doesn't move.

JOLEY 18. I don't know.

STONE. Why?

JOLEY 18. I don't know if I can.

STONE (*reassuring*). I want you here.

JOLEY 18. Do you?

STONE. Yeah, I do.

JOLEY 18 (*reassuring herself*). It's all right, then. (*Remains still.*)

STONE. What's the matter?

JOLEY 18. Absolutely nothing.

STONE (*extending his arm*). Come here, then.

Joley 18 walks toward Stone. Lights down.

Day. One week later for Joley 14, but the same evening for Joley 18 and Stone who are still on the roadside on the other side of the stage, propped against Stone's car. The lights are down on the couple, but up on Joley 14, sitting in a rocker on her porch. She isn't calm; she's anxiously waiting. She looks out at the swamp. Enter Lily.

JOLEY 14 (*hesitant*). What is it? (*Lily is silent.*) What's the matter?

LILY (*slowly*). They're gone.

JOLEY 14. Who?

LILY. Those boys . . . those God-fearing . . . perfect boys.

JOLEY 14. Who?

LILY. Your schoolmates. Ray and Jo-Jo.

JOLEY 14. What are you talking about?

LILY. In the same river . . . this one . . . the one that surrounds us, and baptized them . . . killed them!

Joley 14 drops to the floor. Lily remains within her own thoughts.

JOLEY 14 (*to herself*). They're . . . drowned.

LILY. I remember seeing them at church . . . with their parents, both their mothers and their fathers. Always there. Perfect.

JOLEY 14. When?

LILY. This morning. They were found.

JOLEY 14 (*shaken*). My God!

LILY. They gotta be in a much better place than this . . . at least . . . that's something good. Good underneath all this evil.

JOLEY 14. Evil? What evil? They drowned, right? You said the river killed them! That river's fierce. It'd take anyone, without any warning.

LILY. There was no drowning. Not a real one.

JOLEY 14. It baptized them, and then it killed them. Accidents happen, Ma. Nature is cruel. Real cruel. And that river's a part of it! It's very mean! We can't explain everything and we're not supposed to. Remember? That's what the pastor always told us. I remember that when I used to go to church. Mysteries, right? We just have to accept them.

LILY (*oblivious*). River did kill them. But it wasn't alone. And I do not accept that!

JOLEY 14 (*sickened*). Who else?

LILY. Couldn't have been a person. Much too brutal and vicious! I will not believe a man had a hand in this!

JOLEY 14 (*quietly*). What happened to them?

LILY. There are certain things that are difficult to forgive.

JOLEY 14. And this is one of them?

Joley 30 emerges from the darkness, and Joley 18 leaves Stone. Both women slowly walk toward the porch where Joley 14 is listening to Lily. Joley 30 has her arms around Joley 18's shoulders. All three Joleys listen intently to Lily's tale.

LILY. This man, fishing early this morning, saw something floating around in the river. A catch of light was on it. Like a raft, but not a raft, something else. And it floated in his direction. This man wanted to see what it was, but he couldn't move. Something frightened him, and he didn't know what it was. So he was still, real still, and allowed that "thing" to float toward him. And it was them. Just real still, quiet, and gently, floating in the river. Bound to some board, with wire, sharp, barbed, wire, wrapped around their necks, real tight, until they were no more. Coiled until . . . every breath they had was gone . . . until they became . . . nothing. Nothing on this earth, in this place, that is.

All three Joleys, numb and silent, listen to Lily's tale. The stage turns red and a fire-red light hits the four women and the stage, and remains with them for a few moments. A whistle is heard off-stage, though no one pays attention to it. The whistle is eerie but not frightening, a spiritual call under the red light. Joley 30 and Joley 18 slowly leave the porch and walk to their respective places. Joley 18 returns to Stone on the other side of the stage and joins him on the ground against the car. He is half awake. Joley 18 leans into him. He accepts her. Joley 30 is standing downstage, away from the porch. The light goes down on the two Joleys, but remains on Joley 14. Lily stays on the porch. Joley 14 walks away from her, down the porch steps to the wire fence. She picks up some of the extra wire. The lights go down on Lily. The only light on the stage is on Joley 14. Enter Guy, who approaches her very calmly. He is still immaculately dressed in his clean, white suit, not a hair out of place.

JOLEY 14. What have you done?

GUY. Nothing unusual.

JOLEY 14. Tell me, Guy.

GUY. What do you want to hear?

JOLEY 14. Those boys.

GUY. The two bothering you. Or who bothered you. No more.

JOLEY 14. No more. Because of you!

GUY. And you.

JOLEY 14. I never wanted them dead!

GUY. But why not?

JOLEY 14. What?

GUY. Why wouldn't you want them gone? To me it all seems perfectly natural. Those boys, those silly, dumbassed boys could never scare you again. And that's what they did, wasn't it? Frighten you? Threaten you? Attack you?

JOLEY 14. They shouldn't be dead!

GUY. How could you say that?

JOLEY 14. How could you not?

GUY. My goodness, Joley. I can't believe what I'm hearing. You defending them, after what they did to you.

JOLEY 14. I'm not defending them!

GUY. You are! I did it for you, Joley. There was no gain for me. You did this to me, Joley. You.

JOLEY 14. No.

GUY. It was my hands, but your mind and spirit. You wanted it too.

JOLEY 14. Never!

GUY. You're denying it now, because you're scared. And you really have no reason to be, but don't lie. Inside, you're glad.

JOLEY 14. No! I'm not! You're sick! Crazy! I can't believe I let myself talk to you! I'm so stupid to have let you in!

GUY. And why did you do it? Why, Joley?

JOLEY 14 (*adamantly*). You forced your way in! Following me, everywhere! Swarming around at night with every fly against the screen door! Never letting me be! Shit! No way could I have stopped you.

GUY. You didn't want to.

JOLEY 14. Well I want you to stay away, now! Are you listening to me, Guy? I never want to see your face around here again!

GUY (*calmly*). No.

JOLEY 14 (*begging*). Please. I want you to go away as far as you could go.

GUY. You know I can't, Joley. Not now. Not after . . . us. After the kind of relationship you and I have now. It's different. You're not going to tell me I forced you into that too? Are you? Joley?

Joley 14 is broken.

GUY. Answer me! You can't put me in the same category as those boys!

JOLEY 14 (*quietly*). No. I did . . . that with you 'cause I wanted to. That's all.

GUY. Just as long as we know where we stand.

JOLEY 14. But I never wanted you to harm them!

GUY. I couldn't let them go, Joley. Not after what they did to you.

JOLEY 14. You let them go at the time!

GUY. That's right.

JOLEY 14. And now?

GUY. That was before.

JOLEY 14. Before what?

GUY. You know. Before . . . us.

JOLEY 14 (*realizing*). And that's what made you do it.

GUY. It's not something one can put into words, easily. Especially a man. But something changed, Joley. That's all I can say. It's not as if I didn't care for you before, and that I didn't want to protect you before. I did. And still do. But something was gained. And it overtook me, completely. You did it, Joley. You did this to me.

JOLEY 14 (*numbly*). Now what?

GUY. Nothing.

JOLEY 14. Nothing? Well, if you don't go, I'll leave! Tonight! And I won't tell you or anyone else where I'm going.

GUY. You'll run away?

JOLEY 14. Yes!

GUY. From this place? From your ma? From me?

JOLEY 14. All of you!

GUY. But why?

JOLEY 14. Because of them . . . Ray and Jo-Jo.

GUY. So why would you run? Unless you feel . . . responsible in some way.

JOLEY 14. It isn't that. It couldn't be. I didn't do anything to them.

GUY. Oh I know, Joley. I understand that's how you feel. But you need to remember where you are. This is such a small town. Folks knowing each other's every move and all. Gossip spreading like wildfire. And you and those boys weren't the best of friends. They made that pretty clear. So just think how it would look. So soon after the tragedy. With you disappearing. It would just look kind of strange. You know what I mean?

JOLEY 14. You think of everything, don't you?

GUY. I try to.

JOLEY 14. Are you sorry at all?

GUY. No.

JOLEY 14. Aren't you scared?

GUY. Of what?

JOLEY 14. Of them! Out there! Waiting to find you! Catch you!

GUY. No.

JOLEY 14. Why not?

GUY. Because there isn't need for concern.

JOLEY 14. Two of "them" were killed, and these people in this place won't let that go!

GUY. I don't expect them to.

JOLEY 14. So you think you could just out-run the sheriff and the cops and the dogs and all the men in this town with a rifle in their hands, hunting down their sons' killer!

GUY. I don't have to run anywhere.

JOLEY 14. They'll find you.

GUY. There's nothing to find.

JOLEY 14. You're talking crazy! Of course, there is!

GUY. Like what?

JOLEY 14. Like the wire! The wire you used, which of course had come from my house! They'll find it.

GUY. This town has only one hardware shop, which has in stock only one kind of coil used for building fences. And every single little house in this little town has an especially razor-sharp wire fence which proudly and specifically is used for the sole purpose of keeping out any living and breathing creature which just doesn't belong there. Creatures like you . . . and me, and now the boys. There's nothing to find, Joley.

JOLEY 14 (*examining his lapel*). Your suit is so white, without a single crease in it. I've never really seen anything so white, not around here. There's no sign of a struggle anywhere on you. And Ray and Jo-Jo could put up a struggle, believe me. But it looks like there wasn't any. No effort. No exertion. It's all so calm and still. Just like the river now. It wasn't before, but it's still now. Peaceful. Accepting. And I'm wondering about those boys, those horrible boys. I'm wondering, what they were thinking. If in some way, they accepted everything. Is that what you did to them, make them accept what was going to happen?

GUY. Why shouldn't they accept it?

JOLEY 14 (*frightened*). Why shouldn't they accept? Ma's such an old gossip but she's the one who told me about it. And she didn't want to believe the person responsible was . . . real. I mean, she thought everything was so terrible and cruel, that it couldn't have been done by a person but by something else.

GUY. Like what?

JOLEY 14. I don't know.

GUY. Animal?

JOLEY 14. No. It was all too neat and clean for an animal's doing.

GUY. Then what?

JOLEY 14. She didn't know! Just something else. Un-human.

GUY. I see.

JOLEY 14 (*searchingly*). You're so still. How could you be so still? I can't understand that.

GUY. You're doubting what's before you.

JOLEY 14. I don't know what to believe.

GUY. Well you tell me, Joley! You've been with me! You know! Am I unreal? Inhuman? Barbarous? Is that how I was with you? Is that what you thought when we were together? Is that how you saw me?

JOLEY 14 (*quietly*). No.

GUY. What do you see now?

JOLEY 14. I can't say.

GUY. You can! You can tell me anything, remember that.

JOLEY 14. Can I?

GUY. I would hope so, Joley.

JOLEY 14. I can only see myself, really.

GUY. So, what are you?

JOLEY 14. Scared. Cold. Sick. And trapped. That's what I am. Trapped.

GUY. Trapped?

JOLEY 14. Yes.

GUY. By me?

JOLEY 14. Not just you. I've felt that way for a long time. Trapped by my mother and this place and myself. But it's deeper now. That's all I meant.

GUY. If that's how you feel, go. Get up, and go. I'd never want you trapped, or unhappy, or scared. That was never my intention.

JOLEY 14. What was your intention?

GUY. I just wanted . . . you. I wanted you to feel loved, and protected . . . safe.

JOLEY 14. Did you think I needed love?

GUY. Yes.

JOLEY 14. How could you tell?

GUY. I just could. If you feel led to, if that would make you happy, and at peace, then, go.

JOLEY 14. So easily? You'd let me go?

GUY. You speak as if I own you, Joley. I don't.

JOLEY 14. I wish I could believe you.

GUY. You should.

JOLEY 14. I know better.

GUY. I'm sorry you feel that way.

JOLEY 14. Do you want me to be grateful to you?

GUY. Gratitude was never a part of this.

JOLEY 14. Because I'm not.

GUY. That's fine.

JOLEY 14. Maybe Ray and Jo-Jo were accepting, and I know you are, but I can't be! (*Guy watches her.*) You always win, don't you, Guy?

GUY. There's nothing here to win.

JOLEY 14 (*numbly*). I did this. (*Guy puts his arms on her shoulders. She shudders but doesn't move away from him. She continues, shaking*) You're so cold! Your fingertips are like pieces of ice!

GUY. Am I? You know, I didn't even realize it.

JOLEY 14. It's strange. It's summer. It's swamp. It's South. And you're cold. It's all . . . strange.

GUY. There are things we can't control.

JOLEY 14. Things like Ray and Jo-Jo and the river and the wire fence?

GUY. And you . . . things like that.

JOLEY 14. What are you? Really?

GUY. What I've always been to you, Joley. Nothing's different. I'm the person who's been watching and waiting for weeks, months, for the right time to approach you, which I finally found, and here we are. I'm your friend. The friend who's not going anywhere, and who knows you're not going anywhere. You know that too.

JOLEY 14. What will you do?

GUY. What I've always done. Watch out for you. Just like any friend would. It's nice, isn't it? Having someone always there, looking out for you.

Joley 14 closes her eyes. A breeze overtakes the two. The whistle is heard. Guy remains standing over Joley 14, his hands pressed into her shoulders. Lights down on Guy. Joley 30 enters.

JOLEY 30. Why don't you say something? Open your mouth! Speak!

JOLEY 14. I can't.

JOLEY 30. Why?

JOLEY 14. I'm afraid.

JOLEY 30. Of him?

JOLEY 14. And me.

JOLEY 30. Why you?

JOLEY 14. He'll think I'm crazy.

JOLEY 30. After what he's done?

JOLEY 14. Doesn't matter. Did you hear him? So calm . . . so cool. And I was the one . . . who wasn't.

JOLEY 30. It's all right to shout.

JOLEY 14. Is it?

JOLEY 30. Sometimes you have to . . . to be heard.

Lights down on Joley 30 and Joley 14 and up on Joley 18 and Stone.

JOLEY 18. My mother told me that there are people put on this earth with no place to go. Meaning people like me . . . and her.

STONE. And me?

JOLEY 18. No, not you.

STONE. And not you. Not us.

JOLEY 18. How do you know?

STONE. Because of this.

JOLEY 18. Whatever "this" is.

STONE. Why can't we enjoy what we've just done?

JOLEY 18. I do. I'm just surprised.

STONE. That better not be an insult.

JOLEY 18. The opposite. I felt like . . . I had a place. Before. With you. It was a nice feeling, that's all.

STONE. Good.

JOLEY 18. What am I to you?

STONE. I don't know.

JOLEY 18. Even now?

STONE. Were things supposed to change after that?

JOLEY 18. Yes.

STONE. Why?

JOLEY 18. It has to be more, now.

STONE. Not everything is so damn wonderful.

JOLEY 18. Don't I know that.

STONE. Don't ruin this.

JOLEY 18. I thought I'd be doing you a favor!

STONE. I thought . . .

JOLEY 18. What? That I'd be so cool about this . . . that this would be so . . . easy and I'd be able to dismiss you after and say, "Thanks for the fuck and ride and I'll see you around!" Is that what you wanted?

STONE (*calmly*). I thought you'd know why I'm here.

JOLEY 18. I don't.

STONE. He did this.

JOLEY 18. Who?

STONE. Him. Him before me. He did this to you.

JOLEY 18. I did it to myself!

STONE. No, you didn't.

JOLEY 18. You don't know me.

STONE. Yes, I do. You want me to adore you.

JOLEY 18. I don't want anything from you!

STONE. It can't be all or nothing, Joley.

JOLEY 18. Why not?

STONE. Because that's not the way it is, despite what he told you!

JOLEY 18. He was nothing.

STONE. He must have been everything. But he's not here. I am. I can't give you everything, but I don't want it to be nothing.

JOLEY 18. You mean me to be nothing.

STONE. You're not nothing.

The lights on stage slowly turn fire red.

JOLEY 18. I'm being followed.

STONE. By him?

JOLEY 18. And the others. You know what that sky is? You know what it's telling me? It's my sign. It follows me! It won't let me go! My mark! Who I am. Who I'm supposed to be. And you know what I see when I look at it? Visions. Lots and lots of visions of used car salesmen and beds that creak in the night, that endless night, and barbed wire and church pews and traveling preachers condemning you to hell, but hey, it ain't so bad, and dope and whistles and silly boys floating down on the Mississippi, but they ain't Tom and Huck, cause they're corpses strapped to their magical raft! Those are my sugar plums dancing in my head! Bloody sheets, bloody water, and blood in the sky! Look at it, and see me!

STONE. I don't see you in that hell.

JOLEY 18. That's where I belong.

STONE. Why?

JOLEY 18. Because that's the place I was meant to be in.

STONE. Let it go, and find somewhere new.

JOLEY 18. I don't trust you.

STONE. Yes, you do. Or else, you wouldn't have been with me.

JOLEY 18. Why should I believe you?

STONE. I care. I can't promise everything, like he did, but I care.

JOLEY 18. It's always there.

STONE. So let it go!

JOLEY 18. I don't know.

STONE. You have to.

JOLEY 18. It's what I know. Home.

STONE. Hell. Not home.

JOLEY 18. My home.

STONE. Not now.

JOLEY 18. But it's me.

STONE. Not completely.

JOLEY 18. I think it is.

STONE. All those sad . . . bad things in your sky . . . is that what you want to be known for? Is that what you want to hold on to?

JOLEY 18. I don't know anything else.

STONE. Maybe you should start looking.

JOLEY 18. I'm here, aren't I?

STONE. But you're still there. No matter how many tire tracks you leave in the dirt, you're still home.

JOLEY 18. I don't want to be there.

STONE. So don't.

JOLEY 18. I don't know how to leave.

STONE. So ask (*to the sky*) *it* to leave. (*Joley 18 is silent.*) Scared shitless again? So where is it? Where are the flames that are gonna burn us both out here? Where's our hell? I'm waiting for it! Daring it! Come on! Let it get us both! Finish us off! We're not doing anything important! We're not doing anything great or wonderful! What contributions are we making to this big wide world of ours? We're small people, you and I! So let it scorch us! Turn us into ashes! Call it out, why don't you!

JOLEY 18. That fire sky is our fence. Yours and mine. It'll burn you and cut you until you're no more if you dare cross it. It divides them from us. We're the small things. The I-love-you-s that are just words with no meaning. Like the rejected, with no names . . . nothing . . . always second and third, never first; dark secrets, the ones never brought home to the folks for Sunday dinner; the ones who should be grateful for what's left over; the ones who stay silent, and are thankful for the shit they have! No. We're not first. We're not the big things. The angels. The pink and white . . . white suits . . . white air-conditioning! The safe. The content. Fuck them! So what do we do? People like us. The world's on fire. Remember? Know who you are. No more. Stop trying to be in. Don't think of crossing that fence! Wander! Create! Cry! Shout! Starve! Screw! Shoot up! Self-destruction? Worry about it when you're dead! Drink till you vomit and tear the lining of your insides till there's nothing left and live! And that's living for us. The "small things."

Stone is mesmerized by the sky and by Joley 18's words. She remains fixed on the hell above them. Stone puts his hands on her shoulders, and grips her tightly. Joley 18 remains still. The stage is fire red with the couple at its center. The lights slowly go down on them. Lights up on Joley 14 on the porch steps. Guy approaches.

GUY. You're alone?

JOLEY 14. Yeah.

GUY. Whatcha doin'?

JOLEY 14. Waiting.

GUY. For me? I'm flattered.

JOLEY 14. I don't want to see you anymore.

GUY. I remember, but I still don't know why.

JOLEY 14. Isn't it obvious?

GUY. Not to me. There's nothing to be scared about, Joley. I'll never be traced to those boys floating on that raft. Never.

JOLEY 14. I know. That's why I'm afraid. Because you're not afraid. And because I'm sorry, and you're not.

GUY. We are different.

JOLEY 14. Who are you?

GUY. A protector. A friend. And I'll always be here for you, Joley.

JOLEY 14. I know you'll never be found out. You can do this can't you? You're not like the rest of us. There are no rules for you. Nothing touches you.

GUY. You've touched me.

JOLEY 14. I don't want to.

GUY. It's already done.

JOLEY 14. Why me?

GUY. Why not you? You deserve this . . . attention just as much as anyone else.

JOLEY 14. I don't want it! I never asked for it! Not from you or Ray or Jo-Jo or Bo! No one! Take it back! I don't want it!

Guy starts to walk away.

IMAGE 1.3. **In the middle of nowhere Stone pleads with Joley 18 to be free of her past.**
Akiva Saltzman as Stone and Charlotte Purser as Joley 18.
Blood Sky, Looking Glass Theatre, New York, October 30, 2003.
Photograph by Tony Knight Hawk.

GUY. Too late. It's yours. It's the only thing that's ever been yours, completely yours.

> *The lights on the stage turn fire red. Joley 14 is left alone. She walks to the fence, and looks at the sky. Joley 18 and Joley 30 join her, stand beside her. All three Joleys look not at each other but straight ahead.*

JOLEY 14 (*terrified*). He'll never leave! Guy will never leave!

JOLEY 30. No, he won't. He's intruded.

JOLEY 18. Like Ray, Jo-Jo, Bo.

JOLEY 14. And I let them in.

JOLEY 30. You didn't.

JOLEY 18. I didn't.

JOLEY 14. So now what? Carry them with me? Know they're always there . . . watching me?

JOLEY 18. And they'll continue to fuck you over.

JOLEY 14. When I look up there, into the sky, and I see . . .

JOLEY 18. Fire.

JOLEY 14. Hot. Summer. Darkness. Quiet. Too quiet. Ma. Bo. Blood. Bloody sheets. Boys. Stupid boys . . .

JOLEY 18. Huck and Tom on crack.

JOLEY 14. Guy. River . . .

JOLEY 18. Hell . . . home.

JOLEY 30. Find a separate place for them.

JOLEY 14. She blames me, you know.

JOLEY 30. Who?

JOLEY 14. Ma.

JOLEY 30. For Bo.

JOLEY 14. I pity her.

JOLEY 30. Good.

JOLEY 14. It's following us. Circling us.

JOLEY 18. Like vultures.

JOLEY 30. It'll stop.

JOLEY 18. I'm afraid it won't.

JOLEY 30. It will eventually.

JOLEY 18. But I never asked for this.

JOLEY 30. No you didn't. She didn't and I didn't. But it's ours. It's become a part of us. Overpower it! Put it in its place!

JOLEY 18. I don't know if I ever will.

JOLEY 14. I think you will.

JOLEY 18. Do you?

JOLEY 30. I know you will.

JOLEY 18. But I have to want it badly enough, right?

JOLEY 30. Why wouldn't you?

JOLEY 14. It's bad . . . but not the only part of us . . . I hope.

JOLEY 30. It isn't.

JOLEY 14. It isn't really home, is it?

JOLEY 30 (*comfortingly*). No.

JOLEY 18. All right then. I believe you. I'll have to.

JOLEY 14. So do I.

JOLEY 18. Now what?

JOLEY 30. Shhh. Just listen.

> *All three Joleys stand listening to the wind, looking into the sky. The fire red light turns a peaceful blue. Lights down.*

The End

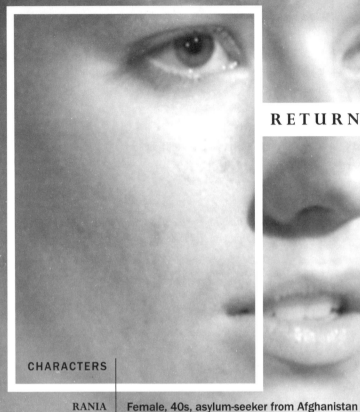

RETURNING

CHARACTERS

RANIA	Female, 40s, asylum-seeker from Afghanistan
AZRA	Female, late 20s, native of Sarajevo, student
MARCO	Male, late 20s, native of Sarajevo, photographer
ANDREA	Female, 40s, native of Sarajevo
CAROLINE	Female, 30s, American, relief worker
TECHNICIAN	Female, early 20s, American, medical technician

SETTINGS	Detention center, New York
	Apartment bedroom, Sarajevo
	Art gallery, Sarajevo
	Medical examination room, New York
	Art gallery, New York

Returning premiered at Johns Hopkins University, Baltimore, on March 3, 2006, with the following cast and crew:

Rania	Tania Hamod
Azra	Julie Sihilling
Marco	Akshay Oberoi
Andrea	Elizabeth Eldridge
Caroline	Elspeth Kursh
Technician	Michelle Brown
Assistant Director	Mitch Frank
Set Designer	Carrie Mossman
Costume Designer	Bettina Bierly
Art Designer	Antony Blaha
Sound Designer	Praem J. Phulwani
Sound Consultant	Vin Scelsa
Producer	John Astin
Director	James Glossman

May 2001. Detention center for asylum-seekers, New York. Rania, an asylum-seeker from Afghanistan, is sitting on a bench in the center of the dark stage.

RANIA (*to the audience*). She looked at me . . . from across the room. She wouldn't look away . . . she had no fear of looking directly at me. She had no fear of my looking directly at her. She wouldn't blink. She wouldn't move. And finally, she spoke. She told me I hadn't cried enough, not nearly enough. There weren't enough rings on the trunk of the tree, and the rings being tears, and the trunk being me. My face didn't have that "burnt" look. The look that comes from . . . too much . . . everything . . . cries, strikes, emptiness, so it's become . . . burnt by everything around it. None of that was there, she said. She saw hope in me, a morsel of it, but it was there, and that wasn't good. I shouldn't have any, I was told. I couldn't have any, or else I couldn't stay. They wouldn't believe me. I wasn't desperate enough. I wasn't hungry enough, or sick enough, or sad enough, or dead enough. How could she have made all those assumptions without ever having spoken to me? But she did. She just knew, she said. So then she offered me the most extraordinary proposition. She offered me her life. Not her body, or even her name, but more severely, herself. Her identity. Her history. Her past. Her present. Her children. Her husband. Her cries. Her strikes. Her hopelessness. Her desperation. She was a story-seller. She sold stories to other detainees so they could get asylum and stay, not return to wherever it was they were running from. I wasn't to worry. She could never run out of stories. She had too many to tell. There would be enough for everyone to go around. And what was wrong with my story, or anyone else's? Why wouldn't it be good enough? It just wouldn't, she said. Who were you mourning for, she asked me. Myself, I told her. No husband? No children? No mother or father? No. Well, not nearly sympathetic enough. She told me her story. How she was a widow from Kabul. How she had been a professor at the university before 1996. Before women had to blacken the windows of their homes so no one would be able to see them inside. Before women and adolescent girls were not permitted to go outside unaccompanied by a male relative. Before women were not permitted to work, so there would be no more female doctors, or teachers, or professors, or government workers. She and some other widows opened a bakery to support themselves and their children. Perhaps they thought a bakery would be the most innocent, unassuming work. What faults could anyone find with a bakery? Closed. Women are not permitted to work. At all. "But how do we feed our children?" she asked. You don't. This was before women had to cover their faces and bodies completely. Before women were not permitted to seek medical help from a male doctor. "But there are no female doctors anymore, so what can we and our children do?" Nothing. Absolutely nothing. No. Nothing is not acceptable. So, many of us go against the law, and leave our blackened houses, unaccompanied, with our sick children, and look for someone who can help, who can do something, or at least say something. But there's no one. So we are helpless. This was all before we were gone, she said. Gone behind those blackened windows. So we could just become . . . nothing . . . no more. Husbands fight in war and die. And then we're left. Left . . . to wait and see what will be of us. Just like this place. A detention, waiting and seeing what will be. And that's where she was, this story-seller . . . here with me . . . waiting and seeing with no one out there waiting for her or for me. With no fear left, just as the husband and the children and the humanity were gone, so went the fear. Maybe that was one good thing, she thought. Nothing to lose. Nothing to fear. And everything to risk. So much so that you find yourself in a place without any recollection of how you arrived or who you were. Her story was my story. Husband and children? I think I had at one time, but no more. So all the stories become rooted into one thick tree trunk. And we become entangled in the branches until no one can distinguish one from the other. And her rings on that trunk become my rings. They're ours, and now . . . they're yours!

Lights up on the other end of the bench where Azra, a visitor, sits.

AZRA. I'm failing you.

RANIA. I don't see that.

AZRA. I do.

RANIA. You're going home.

AZRA. And you're here.

RANIA. You didn't have to be here.

AZRA. Yes, I did.

RANIA. How are you connected to this place? You aren't.

AZRA. Neither are the others.

RANIA. You mean the immigration lawyers and law students and clergy and anyone else who fits that sympathetic description? You don't.

AZRA. I'm not sympathetic?

RANIA. No.

AZRA. Then explain why I'm here. Why I've been coming here.

RANIA. You tell me.

AZRA. Why now? You've never asked me why I've come all these months.

RANIA. Now you're leaving, so this is my chance. Earlier, it didn't matter. I could speak to you about politics and books and articles and art and films and the air outside these walls. That's what I missed. That's what I needed. That's what mattered. Not asylum, or law, or family, or home. What home? But you're returning to one, and now I want to know. Because all of the above doesn't matter . . . now . . . at this moment. So why visit a detention when no one's detaining you?

AZRA. I needed to feel . . .

RANIA. Confined?

AZRA. A piece of it, yes.

RANIA. Why? You're not chained to a bench. You can have the sun on your body anytime you want it . . . anytime it's there. So why want a piece of this darkness . . . this confinement?

AZRA. I wanted to help.

RANIA. We're not strangers, Azra. You've spoken to me. You've been here, faithfully, weekly . . . how could a conversation with a stranger from a strange country, other than your own, who has no connection to you whatsoever, help me?

AZRA. Doesn't it?

RANIA. You know it does. But that's not why you came. Is that what you told the charity, that you wanted to help? I'm sure you did. But that's not why people come, why they do things like this with people like this. People like me. They do for another reason. This gnawing reason inside. It's not about me. Yes, I accept your pity and compassion. I welcome it, actually. But that's not why you've come and I want to know why.

AZRA. It sounds as if you already do.

RANIA. I don't know what gnaws you inside. I never asked you. It never mattered who you were, as long as you were here.

AZRA. You know where I'm from.

RANIA. I know you're going home to Sarajevo.

AZRA. That should be your answer, then.

RANIA. I know you've had tremendous good fortune. That you were sponsored. Brought here to university. Finished. Worked for the university. That you've stayed . . . legally with your own name and your own identity. And that you've chosen to leave. And that you can walk out that door today.

AZRA. You resent me?

RANIA. No. Well, yes, maybe a little bit. You were lucky.

AZRA. And that makes you unlucky.

RANIA. Perhaps. Well, look at where I am. Yes, unlucky.

AZRA. I don't know why people do this. I mean, I know why, but don't they . . . you . . . think of the consequences if you don't do things correctly? If you don't follow what's meant to be followed? Didn't you know this could happen?

RANIA. Should it have mattered?

AZRA. I don't know what it was for . . . look at where you are.

RANIA. I don't need to.

AZRA. Is this better?

RANIA. So the hope goes too . . . along with your leaving.

AZRA. I didn't mean it that way.

RANIA. It's your chance to be honest with me.

AZRA. I suppose that's it.

RANIA. And what would you benefit? What would I benefit?

AZRA. I just want to know what you know . . . what you see . . .

RANIA. What I see?

AZRA. Don't you wonder . . . what will happen? Where you'll be?

RANIA. No.

AZRA. Why not?

RANIA. Why should I?

AZRA. Because it would have all been for nothing!

RANIA. Is that what you see?

AZRA. Yes.

RANIA. You think I'll get sent back?

AZRA. I don't know.

RANIA. I don't think it matters anymore.

AZRA. You're giving up.

RANIA. Is that what I'm doing?

AZRA. I don't want you to do that.

RANIA. Don't worry. You can walk away from your charity work with me with a clear conscience. You did a good thing.

AZRA. That's not what I'm looking for.

RANIA. Did you get to choose me? Is that how it works?

AZRA. What am I doing?

RANIA. I don't know.

AZRA. I'm afraid for you.

RANIA. Thank you.

AZRA. I don't want you to be alone.

RANIA. I already am . . . and what would be so wrong with that?

AZRA. I feel guilty.

RANIA. I know you do. I know that's why you've visited me . . . why you've done this. I see you, where you're from, how you arrived, and I know how you feel.

AZRA. I don't understand! Why imprison someone who just wants to be free?

RANIA. I'm the wrong person to ask. But what did I think would happen? Right? I didn't follow any rule. But let's remember, look at the rules I had to follow, and then ask yourself what else was there for me to do. What other possible choice could there have been?

AZRA. None.

RANIA. That's right.

AZRA. I remember when I was traveling to get here. It was about eight years ago. And I remember going through the airport in Switzerland, and I remember this little man. Why do I say "little man?" Was it because of his stature? No. It has nothing to do with any physical characteristic. He was just . . . no one. Nothing. I don't really mean he was nothing, but that's what he was . . . what his place in the world was . . . nothing. And he was with this . . . this little family of his . . . coming from this place . . . I guess it could have been any place. And they were stopped at immigration. And I remember this officer saying to him, "But sir, this isn't you. This isn't your passport. This isn't your identification. This isn't you." And this man started to scream. And he kept on screaming . . . nonsense. No words. Not real words. Not any real language . . . but just cries. That was the worst sound I had ever heard. It's strange. It touched me just as much as what I saw in Sarajevo . . . just as much as leaving my home . . . my family . . . my boyfriend. This was a stranger, and he pierced me, just as much as anyone or any place intimate to me. And I wondered why. I wondered what power this little man had over me to do that. But the officer kept saying, "This isn't you." And it was only for about two or three minutes. I saw this, and I wondered, how far they had come, and how close they were. And what it takes for someone to do that . . . strip your own identity away, to become . . . nothing. To be told, "This isn't you."

RANIA. Do you know?

AZRA. Now I do. I wonder where he is now.

RANIA. Probably in the same place I am. Maybe I'm him.

AZRA. You're not nothing.

RANIA. Neither was he.

AZRA. He had no identity.

RANIA. Neither do I.

AZRA. Maybe none of us do.

RANIA. You're not "us."

AZRA. Can't I be?

RANIA. You want so much to be confined, on your terms.

AZRA. I don't know how else I'll be accepted.

RANIA. There's nothing wrong with living. With being free.

AZRA. I wish you knew that feeling.

RANIA. So do I. I wish I could remember who I was before all this. I wish I could have someone look at me and say, "But this isn't you." And if I did have someone say that, then I could ask, "So who am I?" And then I would know.

Azra reaches over to Rania and kisses her gently and lovingly on the cheek.

RANIA. Go home now.

AZRA. You're letting me go?

RANIA. Letting go? Like what you let go?

AZRA. But what I released is not completely gone.

RANIA. But it's gone for me. Whatever "it" is.

AZRA. "It?"

RANIA. A person or a place. For me, perhaps both.

AZRA. When do you know this feeling . . . this person . . . or place is gone? Really gone?

RANIA. Are you numb now?

AZRA. No.

RANIA. And you never were. He's with you. He's still with you, even now, even though you left. I think someone has to be overwhelmed—physically—in order to let go of something or someone. But how do you know it is completely gone? Do you have to be numb? Do you have to lose your voice, your breath? Lose control when you speak to that person or hear from that person? And once you go through that "spiritual convulsion" have you let go? I think it takes something so tremendous, so overpowering, so physical . . . to finally . . . let go.

AZRA. Your hands are open. You always sit with your palms upward.

RANIA. Always.

AZRA. But you're not praying.

RANIA. I never do. I never have. I just . . . let go . . . of everything . . . everything that's closed, everything that was . . . is gone. I don't want it anymore. Stripped bare, until there's nothing left.

AZRA. Not nothing! (*Rania is silent.*) I know they'll let you stay. Why shouldn't they, right?

RANIA (*in disbelief*). Why wouldn't they?

Azra rises to leave. Rania is left on the bench. Azra walks to exit and stops.

AZRA. He wasn't nothing . . . that man I saw. He wasn't no one. Neither are you.

Lights dim.

PART 2. Sarajevo

June 2001. Bedroom in Sarajevo. Azra has moved from the bench in New York to this bedroom. On the walls hang black-and-white photographs of scenes of war. A single imposing photo of an avenue under siege is in the center of the upstage wall. Azra sits on the bed at the center of the stage. She is undressed.

AZRA (*to the audience*). I remember seeing absence. A very visible absence. A desolation. An emptiness that said, "We're not all here. Some are missing." There was no greenery. No trees. They had all been cut down and thrown into the fire to re-create the most basic elements that were taken away. I could feel the sun beating us down. There was no wall. Just the sun and us. No veil. Nothing to hide from. Though I felt hidden already, after being a fortunate one who was "away from all that" . . . badness . . . madness . . . I wasn't there. But I heard stories from others who were. And I too watched the footage and saw the photos. But I wasn't there. Don't ask me where I had been. I don't care. I just know, I wasn't there. We were returning . . . me and others like me. We too had been absent, but were coming back. We peered out from the plane's windows to look at . . . absence . . . desolation . . . the earth . . . just earth. Nothing on top of it. Too much underneath it. Just copper-colored fire, by itself. Everyone was so eager to see . . . something . . . nothing . . . everything. No one could speak. What could be said? "I'm back?" "Welcome me?" "Forgive me?" You see, I need forgiveness. How will you receive me now? With weariness? Hatred? Envy? I don't know how it was, and I won't pretend to know. That's yours. You'll own it. You'll own your own grief, fright, hunger, cold, loss. I won't take it from you. I haven't earned it. It's not mine. It doesn't belong to me, and it never will. Perhaps you'll inspire me. I can't inspire you. What will you say to me? Who will I be to you now, after all that? (*The lights go up on the body next to Azra—Marco, also undressed.*) I saw Jasna the other day. We hadn't seen each other since before I left. Before the war. I didn't know if she wanted to see me. Like I didn't know if you wanted to see me. But she did, as you did. I was relieved. We met in the old part of the city, at the cafe. It looked the same, but not the same. We cried, and walked. We took the tram to our old school, but it had been bombed and all the trees were missing. It was so empty. It was strange. There was a yellow school bus parked, but it was burnt. We walked to her building. "It doesn't look so bad," I said as we were walking nearer. She said, "Oh yeah? Turn around." I did. It was burnt, half gone. We went upstairs and inside. We sat, and then she told me things about herself, terrible things. I hated myself, listening to her. I thought, "I should be saying these things too." But I couldn't, because I wasn't there. She was raped, and then she was held, and then she was released, and returned home. She couldn't keep it. You know, that's why they held her. But she got rid of it when she got away. The only thing I could say in response was, "So then what did you do?" What a stupid thing to say! She asked me to look out her window. There was a building across the street. She told me, "Well, I went across the street, and climbed to the roof, and wanted to jump." But she didn't. She couldn't. She turned away. What could I say then? I just listened. But it wasn't the same.

MARCO. How could it be?

AZRA. "That's terrible," I finally said to her, much later. "Oh, I just wanted you to know," she said. She just wanted me to know.

MARCO. You should.

AZRA. Why?

MARCO. They're definitions . . . what people say to you . . . what people see. They're us and you.

AZRA. Not me.

MARCO. Yes, they are.

AZRA. But I left.

MARCO. You weren't the only one.

AZRA. I'm the only one in this bed who did.

MARCO. It was right, for you.

AZRA. Was it?

MARCO. I can't carry that burden for you.

AZRA. Why did you let me come?

MARCO. Why not?

AZRA. Because I left.

MARCO. Don't ask me to recite my ten reasons for fucking you.

AZRA. Only ten?

MARCO. Curiosity.

AZRA. What number is that?

MARCO. I wanted to see.

AZRA. What?

MARCO. Not you. Of course, you. But not like that. Me. Or rather, me with you. It was for me. I wanted to photograph you.

AZRA. You already have photos of me.

MARCO. From before. Not afterwards. I'd like to include you in my exhibition.

AZRA. Why? Your exhibition is about the war. I didn't think you saw me as a part of that.

MARCO. I don't.

AZRA. Then why include me?

MARCO. It's about a part of me. Or a part that was me.

AZRA. You haven't decided which tense you should use when speaking of "us."

MARCO. Not yet.

AZRA. So I'm here as your model. I don't know how to take that.

MARCO. Any way you want. And your reasons?

AZRA. Too many to count.

MARCO. Beyond this room. (*Rising*) I would hope. (*Begins to dress.*)

AZRA. You're not angry?

MARCO. About us? No.

AZRA. At least if you were angry, I'd know you still cared.

MARCO. You should have stayed here. At least you wouldn't have had so much time to think.

AZRA. I often wondered . . . about here . . . and you.

MARCO. Wondered? That's very generous of you.

AZRA. That's not what I meant.

MARCO. All I know is that before . . . all this . . . you and I slept in the same bed but it was as if I were never there. Here I was, in this place, of destruction, where the human spirit was infringed upon in the most . . . bizarre way. Yet, you were never concerned about the status of that body that lay next to you in this bed, and that to me is amazing.

AZRA. I could see everything else. I could listen to everyone else's story, and be saturated with everyone else's bloody photos and films. But not you. I couldn't listen to your stories or see you. Not you. I didn't want to see you that way.

MARCO. But it was me, and my stories, and my (*pointing at the wall of photos*) bloody photos. But understanding that would have been too close for you.

AZRA. It's not about me.

MARCO. Everything's about you.

AZRA. I wanted to keep you, as you, before this.

MARCO. I think it's rare to have the option to decide what you want to see and what you don't want to see. What you'll keep and what you'll lose. When you leave and when you return. That's a lot of freedom.

AZRA. I don't regret it.

MARCO. So you shouldn't.

AZRA. You could have had that freedom too.

MARCO. I couldn't have left. You know that.

AZRA. Other people did.

MARCO. Like you.

AZRA. Like me, and others.

MARCO. I'm not the others.

AZRA. You're not me.

MARCO. When was I you?

AZRA. Before the war.

MARCO. You finally said it!

AZRA. You don't remember?

MARCO. I'm not you.

AZRA. Because I have nothing to prove.

MARCO. And I do?

AZRA. Yes, people like you.

MARCO. Don't!

AZRA. Why?

MARCO. Because you don't know what you're talking about.

AZRA. Lucky me. I'm glad I don't have to know. I'm glad I'm never a question. I wonder about people like you. Half of one. Half the other. Not completely one and not completely the other. I think I would have to prove myself too if that were me. But in the end, after all this . . . who's left watching you?

MARCO. I don't need approval. That's not what this was about.

AZRA. But I wouldn't blame you if you did. That's all I'm saying. I understand why you stayed. That's all.

MARCO. I don't know what I'm supposed to do with you.

AZRA. Nothing.

MARCO. What did you do while you were away?

AZRA. Something I had never done before.

MARCO. Did you get married?

AZRA. No.

MARCO. Did you have a baby?

AZRA. No.

MARCO. Those are the only ones I care about.

AZRA. I stopped. I stepped back. I rewrote my own history . . . which I think is a rather extraordinary thing to do . . . ridding people, silencing yourself, so, perhaps, we're left to think that we were imagined, that there was never an "us." We were never born, so we never died. We never were. I could wonder, but I couldn't say it aloud. Then it would be real.

MARCO. And what's this?

AZRA. I didn't like what I wrote.

MARCO. And you hold all the endings?

AZRA. Haven't you learned? You of all people? There's no such thing. Nothing's finished. Especially not here.

MARCO. Did you expect some sort of loyalty all that time?

AZRA. Not a physical one.

MARCO. Is that how you justified it?

AZRA. I was lonely.

MARCO. You'll find no sympathy here.

AZRA. I guess I'm pretty low on your "suffering barometer."

MARCO. You are.

AZRA. Who's keeping track?

MARCO. I am.

AZRA. Is that all you have left?

MARCO. I hope not.

AZRA. You were trapped.

MARCO. Yes.

AZRA. I felt that, while I was away. I felt your imprisonment, so I needed to feel mine.

MARCO. You were free.

AZRA. Imprisonment through someone else. A woman. An asylum-seeker, in detention, without a home, and without a family. Nobody. As if I were somebody. "I want to help," I said to those who had helped me, and took me away from this place. That was their helping me, taking me away, to feel safe and free. But once I was safe and free I wanted to see imprisonment. To feel it. They sent me to her, whom I visited in prison every week. And I heard her stories, and felt her loss, her imprisonment. I never spoke. I only wanted to hear and to feel. I wanted to feel you.

MARCO. That's not the same.

AZRA. I know that now.

MARCO. Where is she?

AZRA. Still there.

MARCO. And you're here.

AZRA. Were you scared?

MARCO. No.

AZRA. I don't believe you.

MARCO. It's amazing! You're away from yourself. You can't believe you're the one in front of the gun, and the one behind it. But you are. You can't believe where you are, and this is happening all around you. But you are in this place, and this is really happening. And you see things, and hear things, cries, screams, shit like that. And then, there's nothing. Silence. And you're not scared, because you're walking through this fire, and you can't feel it. You have to look at your limbs to see if they're still there, because you can't feel them anymore. You can't feel anything anymore.

AZRA. That's frightening.

MARCO. No. That's power. You've won. You've dared it, and you've won. You dared all the bad to come and get you, and it did. So nothing could ever scare you again.

AZRA. Your camera was your gun.

MARCO. And I came out unscathed.

AZRA. Did you?

Beat.

AZRA (*continues*). If you could feel all that (*looking at the photos on the wall*), maybe you'll feel us.

MARCO. But they're not you.

AZRA. I need forgiveness.

MARCO. From me?

AZRA. Here is you. What's happened is you. What I was, is you. So, yes. You're the only one who can absolve me.

MARCO. I can't.

AZRA. Why not?

MARCO. It's not my place.

AZRA. I'll appoint you.

MARCO. I don't want it.

AZRA. You're so removed.

MARCO. And I can't get back.

AZRA. I think you can.

MARCO. I don't know if I want to go back.

AZRA. You can't stay where you are.

MARCO. Why can't I?

AZRA. It's not you.

MARCO. It's who I am.

AZRA. Who you've become.

MARCO. What's wrong with that?

AZRA. Everything. How can you let nothing touch you?

MARCO. It's survival.

AZRA. It's death.

MARCO. You wouldn't know.

AZRA. I'm glad. I still need forgiveness, but I'm glad I don't know.

MARCO. If you don't know, what can I say to you?

AZRA. What you used to say.

MARCO. There is no "used to!" Nothing can be the same!

AZRA. So why do this? To add me to your collection of horrors?

MARCO. I just needed to see.

AZRA. And now you do.

IMAGE 2.1 **Azra seeks Marco's forgiveness for abandoning him and Sarajevo.**
Akshay Oberoi as Marco and Julie Sihilling as Azra.
Returning, Johns Hopkins University, Baltimore, March 3, 2006.
Photograph by Mark Mehlinger.

MARCO. I always did.

AZRA. And what about what I think?

MARCO. I don't care.

AZRA. Because I don't know what it was like! Because I wasn't here!

MARCO. It's not your punishment.

AZRA. Oh yes it is!

MARCO. Then it's self-inflicted. You should go back to New York.

AZRA. Why?

MARCO. Because you don't belong here anymore. It's not yours.

AZRA. That's a terrible thing to say to me.

MARCO. You've been waiting for it. Waiting for someone to give you permission, that it's all right for you to be back there. That you didn't have to come back.

AZRA. But I wanted . . .

MARCO. What?

AZRA. You know what!

MARCO. No. Tell me.

AZRA. You're a real bastard sometimes!

MARCO. All the time! So tell me.

AZRA. You. Not my family, not anyone else, but you. There.

MARCO. So you saw me. We had . . . something. Now you can go home, wherever that is.

AZRA. You can't forgive me for leaving, can you?

MARCO. No, I can't!

AZRA. If you had gotten that visa, you would have gone too!

MARCO. Of course I would have! There! I said it!

AZRA. But you couldn't get one.

MARCO. No. Maybe I'm envious.

AZRA. There's nothing to envy.

MARCO. Oh, I finally see that now. Maybe that's why I needed this . . . to know . . . the prize wasn't so great, after all.

AZRA. What exactly do you see?

MARCO (*picking up his camera*). Someone I loved, who left. And missed . . . everything. You missed out on seeing people at their best and at their worst. And you say you're glad you did. How can you say that? I saw everything. And now I am one up on those who didn't, people like you. You're looking at me, and you're seeing this . . . absence of feeling, someone who needs to be saved, someone who needs to be humanized again. But you've got it all wrong. Humanity wasn't lost. It was gained. In this place. We shared everything. People like us. We wanted to live and save this place. And we fought and documented this because we wanted to live together, and wanted it to be remembered. It was very simple, you see. We just wanted to be together. What's so dehumanizing about that? I know what happened along the way. I see what's left. I see who's here and who's gone. That's terrible. But I saw it. I was here. And you weren't. And that's terrible. That's all. Leave it alone. Leave us alone. We don't need your salvation or your apology.

AZRA. Is that what you see?

MARCO. Yes.

AZRA (*moving closer to Marco*). Even from here? From this exact place?

MARCO. That's all I see.

Marco begins to take photographs of Azra.

Lights dim.

PART 3. The Photograph

July 2001. Sarajevo Art Gallery. The stage is now an art gallery exhibiting Marco's war photographs. The photograph of the avenue under siege is at the center of the images. Andrea, a visitor to the gallery sits on a bench, centerstage. Marco, carrying his camera, approaches Andrea who is staring fixedly at a photograph of Sniper Avenue.

MARCO. You're taken with this particular piece.

ANDREA. Yes.

MARCO. Why?

ANDREA. You can't hide from it. It forces you to see, even when you don't want to.

MARCO. Oh.

ANDREA. That's not a good enough answer?

MARCO. I was just hoping you'd attribute your reaction to the technique, the lighting . . .

ANDREA. The photographer?

MARCO. That too.

ANDREA. I thought I was.

MARCO. It sounded as if you were captured by its size rather than its substance.

ANDREA. If I've been sitting here for two hours, which I have been, I would think that would be a compliment to the photographer.

MARCO. Thank you for the compliment.

ANDREA. I knew it was you.

MARCO. How?

ANDREA. Besides me, you've been the only person here every day since the opening. You see people see your work. You watch them. Try to guess what they're thinking. Receive their nods of approval. Thank them profusely for their compliments. Ignore their criticisms.

MARCO. Which have been very few.

ANDREA. I know.

MARCO. But I've never seen you before. And you say you've been here every day?

ANDREA. Why should you notice me?

MARCO. Excuse me?

ANDREA. No. I didn't mean for that to sound so harsh, but just . . . the way I see it. I'm not a critic, or a gallery owner, or an editor, or a celebrity, or anything much. That's all.

MARCO. And now I feel terribly guilty.

ANDREA. Don't. And I'm not in here because it's air-conditioned and this is one of the hottest days we've had . . .

MARCO. I wasn't thinking that!

ANDREA. But if you were . . .

MARCO. Which I wasn't.

ANDREA. It wouldn't matter.

MARCO. Why do you want to hide?

ANDREA. What?

MARCO. You can't hide from the piece. You said so yourself. So why would you want to hide from it?

ANDREA. I said that? I was hoping you weren't listening.

MARCO. You didn't answer my question.

ANDREA. I don't know if I can. I can't understand you.

MARCO. The photograph?

ANDREA. No. That's very clear. I can't understand you, or rather, someone like you.

MARCO (*defensive*). Like what?

ANDREA (*points to the photograph*). Like this! Why this?

MARCO. The subject?

ANDREA. The "subject?" It's a much safer way than saying "the shooting," "the killing," isn't it? It's easier to swallow, I suppose.

MARCO (*rises to exit*). Thank you for coming.

ANDREA. Explain this to me, please! I'm a novice, you see. I know nothing about pictures, photographs. So I'm giving you an opportunity to teach someone who knows absolutely nothing but is genuinely interested in your work. What's wrong with that?

MARCO (*stops*). What do you want to know?

ANDREA. Do you consider yourself an artist?

MARCO. Yes.

ANDREA. Do you appreciate beauty?

MARCO. Of course.

ANDREA. So how could you have done this?

MARCO. Not everything is beautiful. Not everything has to be. Not everything should be.

ANDREA. There are so many other "subjects" you could have photographed.

MARCO. That's true. But they're not this.

ANDREA. This is not beautiful.

MARCO. It's not supposed to be.

ANDREA. You were there.

MARCO. Yes.

ANDREA. What were you doing?

MARCO. This.

ANDREA. You weren't waiting for anyone across the street?

MARCO. Would that have made a difference?

ANDREA. You must have been very young . . . a teenager. How could your parents have let you out during this?

MARCO. They couldn't have stopped me.

ANDREA. You couldn't hide from this?

MARCO. No one could. It was right there, in front of us. It demanded that we pay attention. No one was allowed to look away. How could I have been hiding out in some apartment basement while this was happening to us? I had to be a part of it.

ANDREA. You already were.

MARCO. I had to be more.

ANDREA. Why?

MARCO. So I could say I was there.

ANDREA. And then you started taking pictures of it?

MARCO. You make it sound as if I were doing something wrong.

ANDREA. You were!

MARCO. It needed to be remembered.

ANDREA. On a wall? Inside a gallery, an air-conditioned gallery, where it's safe from the stifling heat, along with any undesirable outside?

MARCO. Anyone can see it.

ANDREA. For a price.

MARCO. Which you're willing to pay. (*Beat.*) What else do you want to know?

ANDREA. Does this thrill you? I mean, watching this? Photographing it? Are you like those people who get excited over catastrophes and tragedies like wars, floods, and train wrecks? Some people do, you know. They just want to see. It may be the most exciting moment of their lives! Does this excite you?

MARCO. I was part of a youth house, at the time of the war. That was when our regular school had been bombed. And so we went to this place to learn . . . everything. They gave the older kids cameras that were donated by some organization. They told us to go out there, and document everything we saw, everything that was happening around us. We had to tell people what was happening, make them see it from our eyes. So we did.

ANDREA. But this is safer.

MARCO. It's years later.

ANDREA. No, not that.

MARCO. Then what?

ANDREA. I can look at it, but I can't hear it, and I can't smell it.

MARCO. You could feel it?

ANDREA. If I want to.

MARCO. Do you?

ANDREA. No.

MARCO. Has it changed, each day, seeing it these past weeks? Do you find something new?

ANDREA. Not new. I just concentrate on a different person each day. I wonder about that person, and his or her family. Why he was out. Whom she was seeing. What was said just before they were cut down. What were they thinking? Why was it so important to cross that avenue? Why couldn't they have just stayed inside? What did they have to prove by crossing that street? Did people realize what would have happened? Did they really believe they would have been protected? There's so much noise! I don't know how safe this really is.

MARCO. Who are you looking for?

ANDREA. Them. I can't find them.

MARCO. Your family?

ANDREA. My husband and daughter. You didn't see them?

MARCO. I'm sorry.

ANDREA. I know they were there. Even though I can't see them, I still look.

MARCO. Why were they out?

ANDREA. My husband's family lived across the street. Unfortunately. He wanted to see if his mother was all right. He insisted on taking our daughter with him. He was sure it would be fine. He said his mother missed her, and needed to see her. But they would be fine. They would be protected. People were being helped across the street. If we stayed inside, we would lose. But if we carried on, and defied them, we would win, or so he thought. But I wouldn't go. But I let him take her. Why did I do that? What kind of horrible person am I to have done that? I believed him. I thought it would be fine because he said so. I always believed him. I was very mistaken. So was he. And they were there and now I'm here, left to look for them, but I don't see them.

MARCO. Then you went outside?

ANDREA. I saw it happen, from my window. And then I did a terrible thing . . . something I regret. I went out, out to the avenue, and there was another man, a photographer, like you. He was there, but he wasn't shot. Just like I wasn't shot. He pulled out his camera, and right next to me, in the crossfire, started taking pictures, one after another, so intently. He wouldn't stop. It was like he was fixed on this. He didn't ask questions. He didn't ask anyone's permission. He just started shooting and shooting like a gun. I couldn't believe what he was doing. It seemed so . . . wrong. It was as if we were breaking some very sacred rule . . . this deep intrusion into something so sacred, and so intimate. So I turned to him, and I started beating him with my fists and screaming. I wasn't even saying words. I just screamed and kept on screaming. I think it was a purging of something . . . of everything. I couldn't stop. I didn't want to. He must have thought I was crazy. Maybe he was even afraid of me. I shocked him, you see. So he stopped, and stepped back, and walked away. That's all I remember of that day. I shouldn't have stopped him. Maybe he saw them through his lens, and I might have had something left . . . something I could have kept. Maybe I do understand you now.

MARCO. As an intruder? Because that's how I feel now when I look at this.

ANDREA. It was necessary for you.

MARCO. And what about you? Do you see me as that man?

ANDREA. I did.

MARCO. And now?

ANDREA. I see myself as that man. I'm the intruder now.

MARCO. You have the right.

ANDREA. I have no right. I wasn't one of them, but I still come every day, and watch. I'm just as bad now, even worse.

MARCO. You were a part of it. You still are.

ANDREA. That right should only be given to the victims and the survivors.

MARCO. We're survivors.

ANDREA. We use that title too loosely.

MARCO. You've lost a lot. I've lost too. Not in the same way you did, but I lost someone because of what brought us to that avenue.

ANDREA. We haven't lost as much as they have.

MARCO. This isn't a contest.

ANDREA. Maybe it should be. Then we would have clearer perspective about who gets what.

MARCO. It's too gray.

ANDREA. Yes, it is.

IMAGE 2.2 **Andrea searches for her husband and daughter in Marco's photograph of Sniper Avenue.**

Elizabeth Eldridge as Andrea and Akshay Oberoi as Marco.
Returning, Johns Hopkins University, Baltimore, March 3, 2006.

Photograph by Mark Mehlinger.

MARCO. What do you do now?

ANDREA. Nothing much. I wake up, go to my job, go home, go to sleep.

MARCO. And you come here?

ANDREA. When my job is over. So you see, it's actually quite normal. Except, it's a different kind of normal. A new normal, for me. (*Beat.*) I should go.

MARCO. I have a car. I could drive you home.

ANDREA. No.

MARCO. Well . . .

ANDREA. Thank you, though.

MARCO. No, thank you.

ANDREA. I didn't do anything.

MARCO. For me you did.

ANDREA. Today is the last day of the exhibition, isn't it?

MARCO. Yes.

ANDREA. So what happens? Do you take this home and keep it in your basement or something?

MARCO. Actually, it's going on tour. It'll be in New York next.

ANDREA. Oh.

MARCO. It'll be back again.

ANDREA. New York. That's good for you, isn't it?

MARCO. It's supposed to be.

ANDREA. At least one good thing came out of this.

MARCO. What?

ANDREA. It made you famous. That's a good thing, isn't it? That's what you've worked for, what you've wanted, right? This gave you your chance, didn't it?

Beat.

MARCO (*unsettled*). Yes.

Andrea starts to leave. She turns to Marco.

ANDREA (*searching*). That's a good thing, isn't it?

Andrea exits. Marco is left looking at the photograph of Sniper Avenue.

Lights dim.

PART 4. Sniper Avenue

August 2001. Radiologist's office, New York. Caroline, wearing a bathrobe, is sitting on an examining table on the dark, sparse stage.

CAROLINE (*to the audience*). I was on Sniper Avenue. Really, I was. I know it's hard to believe, but it's true. Me. I never thought I would . . . could go to places like that. Perhaps you don't know what it was. It was this street in Sarajevo, a city in Bosnia. I was there, after the war. They had a war, you know, and I was there. Do you wonder why? Are you looking at me and wondering what could have possibly been my connection? I'm sure that's what you're wondering. I was actually working there. Rather adventurous-sounding, isn't it? I mean, it isn't what people usually do. Not many people. I was with a relief organization. It provided support for women. We helped them a lot. They needed a lot. One in particular. She had lost her husband and daughter while they were trying to cross Sniper Avenue. Her story, her voice, stays with me, even now. Back here, people thought I was crazy to go. My friends thought I'd come back in a box, or come back without a limb. I didn't. Instead, I got hooked. I wasn't afraid of anything, you see. Nothing shook me. Affected me, yes, but not frightened me. There's a difference. Cool, but not cold. But after that, they sent me to other places. Each one worse than the other. But still, nothing. I wouldn't blink. It wouldn't touch me, not personally. I would sympathize with whoever was facing the gun, but I never thought it would be me. And it wasn't. I knew it would never be me. It was as if I were being protected. Like I was a little taller than everyone else, and I could see what was coming before anyone else, and I could jump out of the way, if I ever needed to, which I didn't. I knew more, saw more, or so I thought. I owned my being that person in that place. It enabled me to be special, above average. I could do something that most people couldn't. Or actually wouldn't. But I did. I never got sick. I never got shot. I never got lonely. I never got scared.

Lights up on a chair and monitor next to the examining table. Technician is performing an ultrasound on Caroline's right breast.

TECHNICIAN. Try to be still.

CAROLINE. I thought I was.

TECHNICIAN. You weren't.

CAROLINE. I'm sorry.

TECHNICIAN. It's all right.

CAROLINE. You're being very thorough, aren't you?

TECHNICIAN. Don't you want me to be?

CAROLINE (*half-joking*). No.

TECHNICIAN. Are you uncomfortable?

CAROLINE. No, yes.

TECHNICIAN. Do you want me to stop?

CAROLINE. You could do that?

TECHNICIAN. If you wanted me to.

CAROLINE. But that wouldn't be a good idea, would it?

TECHNICIAN. It's best to finish what we started.

CAROLINE. I suppose. But do something for me.

TECHNICIAN. What?

CAROLINE. Don't tell me if you see anything bad.

TECHNICIAN. I can't tell you anything.

CAROLINE. Why? Do you see something?

TECHNICIAN. No! I shouldn't have said that. But I'm really not supposed to say. Let the doctor read it.

CAROLINE. But you've done this before?

TECHNICIAN. Many times.

CAROLINE. So you know what you're looking for.

TECHNICIAN. I just want to be exact for a clear reading.

CAROLINE. I suppose that's good.

TECHNICIAN. This is your first ultrasound?

CAROLINE. Yes. Have you ever had one?

TECHNICIAN. No.

CAROLINE. Because you're too young?

TECHNICIAN. How old are you?

CAROLINE. I turned thirty-two last week.

TECHNICIAN. Happy Birthday.

CAROLINE (*somber*). Thank you.

TECHNICIAN. Thirty-two's young.

CAROLINE. Is it?

TECHNICIAN. You don't feel young?

CAROLINE. Not anymore. My doctor ordered this. He found something . . .

TECHNICIAN. It's probably nothing.

CAROLINE. What do you see?

TECHNICIAN. Nothing! It's usually nothing.

CAROLINE. You're just saying that.

TECHNICIAN. I'm not.

CAROLINE. I have a bad history, you see. A family history of breast cancer.

TECHNICIAN. But you're young.

CAROLINE. Does that matter?

TECHNICIAN. I think so.

CAROLINE. Do you have anything in your family?

TECHNICIAN. Insanity.

CAROLINE. Really?

TECHNICIAN. No. Well, nothing out of the ordinary.

CAROLINE (*devastated*). I feel horrible.

TECHNICIAN. Don't.

CAROLINE. Did you ever feel that nothing could ever touch you?

TECHNICIAN. No.

CAROLINE. Why?

TECHNICIAN (*searching*). I don't know. I just never felt . . .

CAROLINE. Safe.

TECHNICIAN. Yeah. I don't think most people do.

CAROLINE. I do. I did.

TECHNICIAN. That's good.

CAROLINE. It was a lie. I actually believed nothing bad could ever happen to me.

TECHNICIAN. It hasn't.

CAROLINE. What do you call this?

TECHNICIAN. More ordinary than extraordinary.

CAROLINE. I've been almost everywhere. And you?

TECHNICIAN. Nowhere.

CAROLINE. Why?

TECHNICIAN. It's actually my fiancé. He's not the traveling type.

CAROLINE. You're getting married? That's nice.

TECHNICIAN. Are you married?

CAROLINE (*sad*). No.

TECHNICIAN. I want to go abroad for our honeymoon.

CAROLINE. You should.

TECHNICIAN. I guess I sound rather dull.

CAROLINE. I'd rather be in your place right now.

TECHNICIAN. All this worrying . . .

CAROLINE. Isn't it valid?

TECHNICIAN. It's understandable.

CAROLINE. Even if it all turns out to be nothing, right?

TECHNICIAN. What makes you do what you do? I mean, it's rather nice of you . . . your work.

CAROLINE. Nice of me or nice for me? Did I do it for them, or did I do it for me? I wonder, now.

TECHNICIAN. It's nice all the same. You were there for people who needed someone at that moment.

CAROLINE. Yes, I was there.

TECHNICIAN. Did you come here with someone?

CAROLINE. No.

TECHNICIAN. You should have.

CAROLINE. Why?

TECHNICIAN. It's just . . . easier. I'd want to be with someone.

CAROLINE. I own it . . . whatever "it" is.

TECHNICIAN. It could still be shared. Whatever "it" is.

CAROLINE. Do you see anything?

TECHNICIAN. No.

CAROLINE. I thought you weren't allowed to say. Are you just appeasing me?

TECHNICIAN. No. Where are you working next?

CAROLINE. Nowhere.

TECHNICIAN. Why?

CAROLINE. I don't feel safe anymore. It's been fine up to now, and now I feel . . . very vulnerable, and that isn't good.

TECHNICIAN. All this worrying . . .

CAROLINE. But still. "It's" gone.

TECHNICIAN. What exactly is this "it?"

CAROLINE. Whatever's been protecting me.

TECHNICIAN. It's still with you.

CAROLINE. I don't think so.

TECHNICIAN. Don't let "this" change everything you believe in.

CAROLINE. I think it's so . . . naïve . . . what I've believed in. You know what I've believed in? I've believed in the absolute asinine notion that if someone lives a certain way, a good way, a contributory way, a compassionate way, everything will be . . . OK. I'm arrogant, aren't I?

TECHNICIAN. No.

CAROLINE. I needed to believe in something, and that's what I've believed in.

TECHNICIAN. There's nothing to be certain of.

CAROLINE. But you know. Don't you? When something isn't right? When something has intruded inside you and has grown and taken over you, so much so that it's not you. It's not your control, that control you've worked so hard to attain.

TECHNICIAN. Hey, don't limit this to a disease. A person can do the same thing to you.

CAROLINE. Not me.

TECHNICIAN. Why?

CAROLINE. I wouldn't let it.

TECHNICIAN. You don't let people in?

CAROLINE. It's not up to me.

TECHNICIAN. It is.

CAROLINE. No. It's as if something has been beaten out of you, so that you've become removed, and you wouldn't recognize it, even if it stood in front of you. You wouldn't feel it, you know?

TECHNICIAN (*sad*). No.

CAROLINE. Lucky you. On more than one count. I was never lonely. I went into places, places I had no prior connection to, and yet, I never felt . . . alone. But here I am, in this place I grew up, with people who've known me my entire life, and I feel this emptiness that comes from such a deep, dark place, that I at this very moment on this table at this time feel completely alone. And that's what this "thing" does to you.

Technician doesn't answer; he is carefully looking up to the monitor screen which now appears on the upstage wall, behind the examining table. It is an actual ultrasound which detects a substantial mass.

TECHNICIAN. You're not alone.

CAROLINE. Do you see anything?

TECHNICIAN (*slowly*). No.

Lights dim.

PART 5

August 2001. New York City Art Gallery. Caroline enters the gallery exhibiting Marco's photographs. Azra has been sitting on a bench at centerstage, looking at the photographs.

CAROLINE. I was there.

AZRA. On the avenue?

CAROLINE. Yes.

AZRA. But you're not from Sarajevo.

CAROLINE. No, but you are.

AZRA. Yes, I am.

CAROLINE. So you were there also.

AZRA. No, I wasn't. I was here.

CAROLINE. Oh.

AZRA. You were working there?

CAROLINE. Yes.

AZRA. Did you like it? It's a stupid question . . . I mean, it was during a war . . .

CAROLINE. Yes, I did like it.

AZRA. How did you like something horrible?

CAROLINE. Horrible and beautiful.

AZRA. Beautiful? How could this (*pointing at the photographs*) be beautiful?

CAROLINE. An unexplainable beauty . . . something . . . deep . . . spiritual . . . a fighting spirit . . . a desperation for more than survival in the literal terms . . . I don't know. If you weren't there, you wouldn't know.

AZRA. It's more mine than yours.

CAROLINE. But you weren't there.

AZRA. I'm from Sarajevo!

CAROLINE. I don't take that away from you . . . I'm just saying . . .

AZRA. How easy it is for you to claim this!

CAROLINE. I don't claim it! It's not up for ownership!

AZRA. It wasn't your home . . . your people . . . your mess! You were just passing through!

CAROLINE. It was more than that to me.

AZRA. Then why aren't you still there?

CAROLINE. I . . . was needed elsewhere.

AZRA. Oh . . . you were needed! You're so invaluable to us, aren't you!

CAROLINE. I'm not going to be judged.

AZRA. The truth's painful, isn't it?

CAROLINE. I didn't have to go . . . I wanted to be there.

AZRA. What invaluable, beautiful deed did you do for people like me? I'd like to know why you . . . of all people were so necessary to the war?

CAROLINE. I listened.

AZRA. You listened.

CAROLINE. Among other things, but that was the most important, I think.

AZRA. Do you?

CAROLINE. I do.

AZRA. That's necessary work?

CAROLINE. Not exclusively, but equally. Sometimes, people just need to be heard. They just need to know that someone cares and is listening and will be there . . . for however long it's possible to be there. Sometimes that's just as important, just as necessary, as everything else.

AZRA. So you wrote a book about your "experience" in the war or something as noble and admirable, and most likely, lucrative?

CAROLINE. No, I didn't.

AZRA. A journalist on the frontline! This would be a great proposal for a grant for a documentary or something! I'm sure you could finally get whatever funding it was you needed . . .

CAROLINE. But I'm not a journalist or a filmmaker or anything like that!

AZRA. The noble relief worker! Are you with the UN? I hear they give great parties. Is that true?

CAROLINE. No, I'm nothing like that. I just worked with this very small church-based charity. It was nothing much.

AZRA. Ah! So is your mission to convert us? Convert me? People like me so I could become like you! Is that why you were over there?

CAROLINE. No, it wasn't like that at all.

AZRA. So you were just being . . . a good person! A generous humanitarian!

CAROLINE. Good? I don't know. You're looking for something more than goodness. I'm not good. Not at all.

AZRA. Then why be there?

CAROLINE. And why be guilty because you weren't? (*Beat.*) You want some sort of justification . . . Well I wasn't a journalist looking for fame, or a relief worker with some tremendous organization looking for admiration. And I really can't answer your question. I actually thought, for a minute, before, that I did go over there for some sort of . . . I don't know . . . point, do you know what I mean? Like I was going somewhere people . . . people from where I come . . . usually don't go. That I was doing something . . . special . . . and that made me special.

AZRA. It did.

CAROLINE. No, it didn't. I realize that now. I'm not . . . extraordinary . . . or special . . . or anything like that. I'm not sorry I was there because it's not about me anymore.

AZRA. I'm sorry I suggested you had ulterior motives.

CAROLINE. I'm not. Maybe I did.

AZRA. You didn't.

CAROLINE. I know that, now. So my conscience is clear.

AZRA. I wish mine, too, could be.

CAROLINE. Don't you see? It didn't matter I was there! I'm back home now, and it didn't matter I was there! Just like it didn't matter you weren't.

AZRA. It does.

CAROLINE. You feel regret?

AZRA. Only for myself.

CAROLINE. So do I.

AZRA. Why?

CAROLINE. For thinking it would matter.

AZRA. It did! I don't know you, but I'm sure it did. You probably don't even realize how much it did.

CAROLINE. And for me?

AZRA. I don't know . . .

CAROLINE. Now where do I go? What do I do?

AZRA. Go on, to the next place. There's always the next war, the next Sniper Avenue, right?

CAROLINE. Sometimes you don't need to go outside your little world to meet that next war. It could wait for you, right in the place you considered home. Where's your home?

AZRA (*pointing at the photo of Sniper Avenue*). Here.

CAROLINE. Really?

AZRA. I understand that now. Though I was away from it, it's me. Only people . . . such as you . . . can understand that. I don't even know you, and I can stand here before you . . . and I know you know what this "home" is like. You could have stayed in the place you were born, never having left, and I'd know you know what this home—hell—is, don't you?

CAROLINE. Yes.

AZRA. That's why you're here now, aren't you? You had to feel it again, because I think you're facing it.

CAROLINE. God, that's what I miss, this mystical, spiritual sense! When I was there, I could bump into a stranger on the street, and this stranger could just look into my eyes and know me inside and out.

AZRA. Whatever it is . . . I think you'll be fine, eventually.

CAROLINE. Eventually? You're a psychic?

AZRA. No, just a stranger on the street.

CAROLINE. Eventually . . .

AZRA. If you can accept that.

CAROLINE. Do I have a choice?

AZRA. Yes. Do you accept it?

CAROLINE. I don't know if I can.

AZRA. None of this was for nothing. You know that. It's you. You're not nothing. I'm not nothing. Those people on the avenue weren't nothing. So how could have all this been for nothing? It couldn't have been, don't you see? (*Caroline doesn't answer, and leaves. Azra is left with the photograph of Sniper Avenue. Marco joins her. To Marco*) What do you see?

MARCO. Where?

AZRA. In there.

MARCO. I don't know.

AZRA. It looks to me you were searching for someone.

MARCO. I was. But I don't know who.

AZRA. My arrogance . . . or rather my hopefulness led me to believe, that it may have been me.

MARCO. Maybe it was. I'm not sure.

AZRA. Maybe I shouldn't have come.

MARCO. But you did. Why?

AZRA. I wanted to see . . . this.

MARCO. Nothing you hadn't seen before.

AZRA. Not in this place . . . not like this. You should be proud.

MARCO. Should I?

AZRA. It's tremendous.

MARCO. Why?

AZRA. Because you brought attention to something so sad and so powerful . . . and you were so young while you were doing it.

MARCO. Through others' pain.

AZRA. Through your own.

MARCO. Well I'm standing here, talking to you, with my face not burned off and my limbs intact . . . What pain do I have?

AZRA. You were the one "in front of the lens and behind it." You should know. I don't.

MARCO. I know you don't. (*Beat.*) What are you doing?

AZRA. I don't know.

MARCO. You're trying so hard to see something that isn't there.

AZRA. It was.

MARCO. But not "is."

AZRA. I think you feel differently. Not know differently . . . but feel.

MARCO. How do you know that?

AZRA. Because I just do.

MARCO. You're taking a risk.

AZRA. I never thought I'd hear you say that to me.

MARCO. But you are.

AZRA (*searching the exhibition*). Where am I?

MARCO. The photo I took in Sarajevo?

AZRA. I don't see it.

MARCO. I didn't include it.

AZRA. I suppose, it wouldn't have fit.

MARCO. Not for this.

AZRA. No, not for this. Who will your next subjects be?

MARCO. Why did you just use that word?

AZRA. Subjects? That's what they are . . . what we are, aren't we?

MARCO. It's easier to say, isn't it?

AZRA. Easier than what they are . . . what they represent.

MARCO. I haven't decided what my next exhibition will be about. Maybe people like you.

AZRA. Like me?

MARCO. The ones that weren't there, but are now. The ones returning.

AZRA. How would we be received?

MARCO. I don't know. That's why I'd photograph you. To see.

AZRA. You'll go back to Sarajevo?

MARCO. Of course.

AZRA. Why "of course?"

MARCO. Because it's where I have to be.

AZRA. Not anymore.

MARCO. Especially now. Don't you want to see what happens next? That can be just as interesting

AZRA. Reconstruction? Politics? Peace?

MARCO. All of it.

AZRA. I didn't think I belonged anymore.

MARCO. I didn't think you did.

AZRA. But now?

MARCO. Perhaps I was wrong.

AZRA. Perhaps we don't work.

MARCO. Maybe we don't work in the same place.

AZRA. We did.

MARCO. Did.

AZRA. Not "do." I should have stayed.

MARCO. This still could have happened, all of it, and we'd still be standing here, looking at this, knowing . . .

AZRA. You're leaving.

MARCO. And you aren't.

AZRA. I didn't say that.

MARCO. No?

AZRA. It can't be the same, can it?

MARCO. No. But that doesn't mean, it can't . . . be.

AZRA (*moving closer to Marco*). Do you see anything?

MARCO. Now I do.

    Azra and Marco kiss.

The End

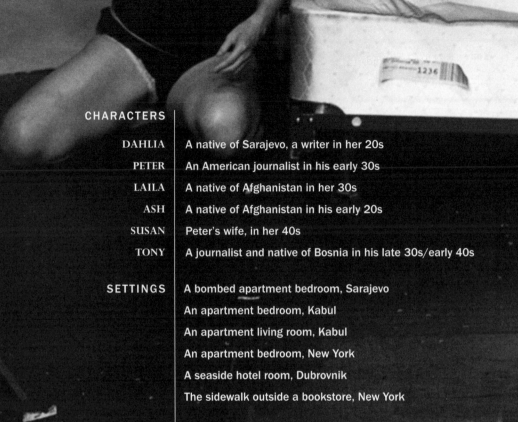

CHARACTERS

DAHLIA	A native of Sarajevo, a writer in her 20s
PETER	An American journalist in his early 30s
LAILA	A native of Afghanistan in her 30s
ASH	A native of Afghanistan in his early 20s
SUSAN	Peter's wife, in her 40s
TONY	A journalist and native of Bosnia in his late 30s/early 40s

SETTINGS

A bombed apartment bedroom, Sarajevo

An apartment bedroom, Kabul

An apartment living room, Kabul

An apartment bedroom, New York

A seaside hotel room, Dubrovnik

The sidewalk outside a bookstore, New York

THE WAR ZONE IS MY BED

The War Zone is My Bed premiered at La MaMa ETC, New York, on October 20, 2007, as part of "Experimenta: A Festival of Plays Celebrating 10 Years of La MaMa's Play Reading Series," with the following cast and crew:

Dahlia	Jenne Vath
Peter	Alexander Alioto
Laila	Sheila Dabney
Ash	John-Andrew Morrison
Susan	Candace Reid
Tony	Jason Howard

Costume Designer	Sally Lesser
Lighting Designer	Federico Restrepo
Set Artist	Mark Keho
Music Composer	Gengi Ito
Sound Designer	Tim Schellenbaum
Production Manager	Julie Rosier
Press Representative	Jonathan Slaff
Director	George Ferencz

Sarajevo. Winter, 1994. An apartment in Sarajevo, empty except for a bed and two hardbacked chairs. The bed is flush against an upstage back wall which is riddled with bullet holes and which reveals patches of exposed brick. The floor is covered with clothes, empty bottles, and ciga-rette packets. There is a door stage right and a glassless window stage left. There are two people under the sheets on the bed. Peter climbs out of bed, picks up his clothes, and dresses while talking to himself.

PETER. You're a walking x-ray. That's how I see you. Though you don't know it. You think you're controlled. You think it's reserve, but it's there: every thought, every emotion, every tear, every regret, every disappointment . . . in yourself . . . others . . . me, especially me. You stand on a higher moral ground, and you look down on us, me. You show . . . every-thing. You give . . . everything. You risk . . . everything. For what? Honesty? Directness? Brutal honesty? The final word? What if I'm not here to listen? What if no one's left to listen? You're supposed to reveal everything. So where's your joy?

Lights up. Dahlia sits up in bed.

PETER. Where's your joy?

DAHLIA. Why do you ask?

PETER (*begins to pack*). Because I can't see it.

DAHLIA. Should you? Is your curiosity about me? Or us? Are you asking if I was unsatisfied by you? Couldn't you have asked me that?

PETER. It was just a question, Dahlia.

DAHLIA. A silly one.

PETER. I didn't think so. Until you made it more than it was intended.

DAHLIA. You don't like my thinking?

PETER. It's your head. You're too much in it.

DAHLIA. Where else should I be, Peter? In yours?

PETER. You're already in mine.

DAHLIA. You let me in.

PETER. My mistake. (*Beat. Dahlia gives Peter a killer look.*) Don't do that.

DAHLIA. What?

PETER. Look at me like that.

DAHLIA. Like what?

PETER. Right through me.

DAHLIA. Is that what I'm doing?

PETER. What you always do.

DAHLIA. Is there something you don't want me to see?

PETER. Too late for hiding.

DAHLIA. What time is it?

PETER. Soon.

DAHLIA. That's not why I asked.

PETER. Was I being egocentric?

DAHLIA (*playful*). When are you not?

PETER. You're angry?

DAHLIA. Yes.

PETER. Oh, so would you like me to go now?

DAHLIA. No. (*Beat.*) I could be joyful for you. (*Dahlia kneels and wiggles her ass at him.*) Is that what you had in mind?

PETER. Not for me.

Dahlia returns to sit on the bed.

DAHLIA. Thank you for your concern. (*Reclines.*)

PETER. It's more than concern.

DAHLIA. Then stay.

PETER. I can't.

DAHLIA. Then take me with you.

PETER. If I were better, I would.

DAHLIA. But you're not.

PETER. I never was.

DAHLIA. Oh. So the good get better, and the bad get worse, and those in between . . . are the most pathetic.

PETER. Something like that.

DAHLIA. I wonder what page I'll be on.

PETER. What?

DAHLIA. Of your lovely book . . . your book of stories. Well that's what you've been doing here these past six months, right? That's what journalists do, right? Report on stories about exciting people like me, caught up in the war. In the mess. In the grime. In the filth. (*Sitting up*) In no heat and no hot water. In missing people. In people who were here and now they're not. In people who become . . . nothing. Become? No. Maybe there were always nothing, so what would it matter to them. But, to you, that would be a different story. You come here to be around people like us. Nothing. So where will I be?

PETER. The book's not just about you.

DAHLIA. It's only about me! We have different faces but the same stories, and out there aren't many of us left. And what is left doesn't feel very good.

PETER. Then you don't like yourself.

DAHLIA. I don't, not really.

PETER. Since the war?

DAHLIA. Since before . . . since during . . . since . . . now, waking up to you today. I don't know. It's hard to remember what we were . . . before . . .

Both react to fragments of war—noise—an explosion from outside the window. The chairs are knocked over. Dahlia hides behind the head of the bed at stage right. Peter joins her. There are sounds of machine-gun fire and trucks pulling up outside the apartment building. Sniper fire is heard from the rooftop above. Men run up the stairs to the apartment above Dahlia and Peter. Peter sees a pack of cigarettes in the center of the room and crawls on his stomach toward it, then freezes at the sound of heavy footsteps coming down the stairs. There is more shooting outside as the trucks pull away. Bombs explode in a distance. Peter reaches for the cigarette pack. It is empty. He turns and faces Dahlia. She lights a cigarette, crawls toward him, and they share the cigarette, listening to the war outside.

DAHLIA. What were you before this, Peter?

Boom. Explosion. Dahlia flips Peter and holds a cigarette to his face.

PETER. You're not making this very pleasant.

DAHLIA. Well, I really don't give a shit right now! Is that what you want "this" to be? Is that what defined us . . . whatever "us" was? Is "pleasant" what defined "this?" This place? Your

IMAGE 3.1 **After an explosion, Dahlia and Peter fight over a cigarette.**
Jenne Vath as Dahlia and Alexander Alioto as Peter.
The War Zone is My Bed, La MaMa ETC, New York, October 20, 2007.
Photograph by Mark Roussel.

reason for being here? Honestly, none of this sounds very pleasant.

PETER. I thought we were pleasant.

DAHLIA. Pleasant? I think of pleasant as being peaceful. And we were never peaceful.

PETER. And you're referring to . . .

DAHLIA (*gestures toward the bed, the bullet holes, and the window*). All of that. Why don't we start with fucking under a shelling?

Peter flips Dahlia and they roll on the floor to stage left. Boom. Shelling.

PETER. I'm excluding what went on outside these four walls.

They roll across the floor at stage right.

DAHLIA. You can't. We come as a package deal. You get the shelling and the sex—I think it's a fabulous deal.

More shelling.

PETER. It's survival.

Dahlia flips Peter over, twisting his arm behind him.

DAHLIA. Which you know nothing about.

PETER. Which I learned from you.

DAHLIA. Then you stole from me! (*Bangs Peter's head on the floor.*)

PETER. What are you talking about?

DAHLIA. The stories . . . my stories! (*Bangs Peter's head again.*) You made them yours! You made "this" story your story!

PETER. In Sarajevo, it's everyone's.

DAHLIA. You adopted it! I was born to it! (*Bangs Peter's head on the floor yet again, returns to the bed, and wraps a sheet around her head like a hijab.*)

PETER. I wanted to bring attention . . . (*Slowly gets up from the floor.*)

DAHLIA. You wanted to be a hero! (*Removes sheet.*)

Peter crosses to stage left, to the foot of the bed.

PETER. No. No one wins. I see that now.

DAHLIA (*desperate*). You wanted to become famous!

PETER. I wanted to write the truth! I wanted to bear witness. I wanted people to know.

DAHLIA. Through your words.

PETER. It didn't matter who was telling this story! But someone had to, and no one was. So I did. But I never took from you. You spoke freely.

DAHLIA. So that's your justification.

PETER. No, but that's what you wanted to hear. It was more than your story.

DAHLIA (*mockingly, imitating a news reporter*). What was it Peter, what was it that made you want to fuck me in the first place?

PETER. Don't do this.

DAHLIA. No. You're leaving, and this is my chance to know. Was it your loneliness? Your fear? My story? Was it me or my story—or our story? Or this war? Was it this war you actually wanted to fuck?

PETER. What are you getting out of this?

DAHLIA. Not as much as you did.

PETER. I met you, first, and then your story.

DAHLIA. How much was your book deal?

PETER. People back home started talking about people like you. Empathizing with people like you.

DAHLIA. Thanks to you. (*Sits on the edge of the bed.*)

PETER. Thanks to someone.

DAHLIA. Feel better?

PETER. No. (*Crosses to his bag.*)

DAHLIA. Did you think your words would ease anything?

PETER. Attention was given.

DAHLIA. Master of timing, Peter. You seem to know exactly when it's safe for you to just ease into a war zone and make a fast run for it before anything really happens to you.

PETER. It was better than never. (*Crosses to the door.*)

DAHLIA. More justification.

PETER. Dahlia, there is nothing else I can say.

DAHLIA. Strange for a journalist.

PETER. I don't have words for this moment.

DAHLIA. Back to stupid, silly words. (*Crosses to stage right and sits at the head of the bed.*)

PETER. You're a writer.

DAHLIA. Was.

PETER. You still are.

DAHLIA. I stopped.

PETER. You shouldn't have.

DAHLIA. There was no point in continuing.

PETER. I don't believe you. (*Sitting next to Dahlia*) I know you value words. You know where they can lead. You know they can serve as the catalyst for something greater, greater than what's happening at the moment. I see through you and I know you think differently.

DAHLIA. Words over people.

PETER. I value you.

DAHLIA. You use me. And I let you.

PETER. I'll miss you.

DAHLIA. How can you miss something you never had? (*Crosses to window and stares out onto the street. Peter stays on the bed.*)

PETER. I had you. (*Crosses to Dahlia and stands behind her.*)

DAHLIA. In a place, very far away, where no one knows you, where you have no past or future, where every action and every word can be attributed to the war, something out of your control. We're false, you and I. You can do what you wish because Dahlia and Peter aren't real.

PETER. We were to me.

DAHLIA. We "were" because you always knew it would be we "were" and not "are" and not "will be." We "were" is easier than we "are." And we are not "are."

PETER. You're giving me a headache.

DAHLIA. Good!

PETER. Why did you stop writing?

DAHLIA. I let you write for me.

PETER. You should have written your own stories.

DAHLIA. I couldn't.

PETER. Maybe later?

DAHLIA. Maybe never.

PETER. Too close? Too much credence if you actually document what happened to you? Give yourself a voice? Would that have made it real for you?

DAHLIA. I never denied what was happening to this city.

PETER. But you don't look at yourself. It's all about what's out there . . . and not in here.

DAHLIA. It's one and the same, can't you understand?

PETER. No, I can't. You're the writer, though you deny it. You're like me. An observer, on the outside, looking in. You never really considered yourself one of them. Them being the powerless, the victims. You? A victim? I don't think so. (*Crosses to the bag by the door on his way out.*)

DAHLIA. Take your stories and enjoy what they bring to you. Don't worry. Guilt-free. You have my permission.

PETER. It would have been someone else.

DAHLIA. But at least it wouldn't have been you.

PETER. And you would have been with him, whoever he may have been. Because he would have been your voice. And that would have given you a little bit of what you were, before this . . . Shit, and that would have been enough. And you would have been standing here, on this day, having the same conversation with him, rather than with me. You said it your-

self. Same story. Same faces. We're one, here. If it weren't I, it
would have been someone else.

DAHLIA. As I would have been someone else?

PETER. I don't know. But I don't think so.

DAHLIA. You're so clean and honest, Peter. Nothing damages your character, does it?

PETER. It's because of her. Her plus me. Plus this. Plus how I'm leaving you. Plus this absence . . . plus this nothing.

DAHLIA. Her? Why don't we give "her," Susan, her name, so we could baptize this fucking moment!

PETER. And you?

DAHLIA. What?

PETER. Was it me, or the thought of getting on that plane with me today?

DAHLIA. That's a senseless question.

PETER. Why?

DAHLIA. Look at yourself! You came, you observed, you wrote, and now you leave. And that's all this moment is about. So, how can I think of myself to you as anything but . . . nothing?

PETER. Why even let me in?

DAHLIA. I hoped for more. There.

PETER. But you knew . . . about . . . her . . . my wife . . . Susan . . . my situation . . .

DAHLIA. Your situation? No. Not really. Not until this moment.

PETER. I can't give more.

DAHLIA. You don't want to.

Peter drops the bag and goes to the left of the bed.

PETER. What's standing before you . . . is a coward. I wrote about events that I was never engaged in, not really engaged in. I wrote from my window, looking down, onto the street. I documented people's trauma, not my own, though I wanted it to be my own . . . a bit of justification as I defend what I've been doing for the past six months. One foot is already out your door. Not as a reflection on you, but on me. I don't want to see you again. I don't want to speak to you again. I don't want to hear your voice again. I don't want to smell you again, or feel your body again. If we were to speak, and the connection would return, I'd lose my inhibitions and imagine myself being with you. But I'm not strong or brave enough to follow my fantasy. So I settle for what I have.

DAHLIA. You're brave enough to admit you're a coward.

PETER. If I had to be you, I wouldn't have survived.

DAHLIA. You don't know that.

PETER. I do.

DAHLIA. You run away from everything and everyone. What are you afraid of?

PETER. Nothing.

DAHLIA (*swipes Peter's passport from his pocket*). Then stay.

PETER. I can't.

DAHLIA (*takes lighter out from panties and lights a flame close to the passport in her hand*). Are you running from me?

PETER. Not from . . . to.

DAHLIA. To what? To heated and happy homes equipped with stupid, smiling faces? To bullet-free walls and houses that still have their roofs above them? To peaceful, bomb-less slumber? To Susan? (*Throws Peter's passport back at him.*)

PETER. I'll miss you.

DAHLIA. Miss me?

PETER. It's something.

DAHLIA. For me? Am I to feel grateful? Is that what's left? After everything? Thank you? It's not enough.

PETER. Do you want me to lie to you?

DAHLIA. Why can't you?

PETER. Dahlia . . .

DAHLIA (*calmly*). Forget it. Forget everything I've said. (*Crosses to the window.*)

PETER. You know I won't.

DAHLIA. Yes, you will, eventually. But I won't.

PETER. Come on! Hit me! Throw something at me! Throw me out! Make me . . .

DAHLIA. Feel something?

PETER. Yes.

DAHLIA. I can't do that for you. Or else, I would have already. You feel me. I know you feel me. I'm not missing because I'm standing right here, before you. Honor my presence, honor us.

PETER. How?

DAHLIA (*moves to Peter and puts her arm around him*). Here's your opportunity. I'll hand it to you. Take your chance now. Take the risk . . . and see with me. See not just for me, but for you. Stay here, and continue our stories. Write about us after the guests have gone home from the funeral. What do the ones left behind do then? Will we learn from our mistakes? Will we trust? Will we be so desperate that we'll trust the wrong people, because the right ones have left? (*Falls to her knees.*) We're not finished . . . you . . . me . . . the people outside these four walls. Your book shouldn't end here.

PETER. You're right. I think you should continue where I left off.

DAHLIA. Why?

PETER. I promised Susan I'd go back.

DAHLIA (*stands up*). What if you had died? You would have broken your promise, wouldn't you?

PETER. I didn't die.

Beat.

DAHLIA. You just did. (*Beat.*) For me. (*Turns away.*)

Peter takes his bag from near the door, looks at Dahlia, heads to the door, opens it, and leaves. He leaves the door slightly ajar, and stands outside, listening.

IMAGE 3.2 **Dahlia is left behind in Sarajevo.**
Jenne Vath as Dahlia.
The War Zone is My Bed, La MaMa ETC, New York, October 20, 2007.
Photograph by Mark Roussel.

DAHLIA. The joy was before you. Not before the war, but before you. But you didn't want to see my joy. You only wanted the sadness . . . for your stories. Yes, there was sadness, tremendous sadness and loss! You liked me . . . as the sad one. It gave you some purpose for being here. Yes, there was great sadness, but also joy, or hope that there may be joy again. How could I stand here before you without that element of hope! But that wouldn't have worked for you. I wouldn't have worked for you. But thank you. For now, your efforts are named . . . heroic. Yes, there was joy. There is joy, even now, even at this very moment. I feel it. It's coming back to me. Perhaps that's something I could write about once you go through that door.

Door shuts completely.

Lights dim.

PART 2. Blackened Windows

Kabul. Winter, 2001. The setting is the same as in Part 1. The bed is center perpendicular to the back wall. Near the door hangs a burqa. Downstage left and right are placed two comfortable chairs. A glass window is blackened. Paintbrushes and cans of paint are sprawled across the floor. Laila and Ash are in bed. Both are naked. Laila awakens, rises, pulls a black slip over her. She goes to the blackened window, takes a paint brush, and proceeds to blacken it further. Ash awakens.

ASH. Is it day or night?

LAILA. I can't tell.

Ash looks at his watch on the floor.

ASH. It's day.

LAILA. If you say so.

ASH. What are you doing?

LAILA. I was afraid we could be seen. It's the law, you know.

ASH. I can't see anything. Come here.

LAILA. No.

ASH. Why?

LAILA. I have to do this first.

ASH. You really can't see anything.

LAILA. That's the way it's supposed to be.

ASH (*turns over*). You're not missing much.

LAILA. Only the sun, any light, rain, gray, blue . . . blue sky . . . black sky—but not a painted black sky—the real black sky . . . light . . . warmth . . . faces . . . eyes . . . just those things.

ASH. It's not that beautiful out there.

LAILA. I wouldn't have any idea.

ASH. Well, I would. And it's not nice.

LAILA. Nice or not. I don't care. But it's something.

ASH. Come here, Laila. (*Laila hesitantly leaves her task and joins Ash in bed.*) You worry too much.

LAILA. It's the truth.

ASH. Then why take the risk? Are you still missing your husband? Missing someone? Is that it? Am I the someone?

LAILA. He's dead. There's no point in missing him now. I miss myself.

ASH. And this brings you back?

LAILA. In a way . . . yes. A little bit. It's a little bit of humanity . . . these times with you. Where I can see not only your body, but mine, and mine with yours. Where I can see myself, despite being in a blackened box. Where I can be touched and can touch and feel and know, that there's an escape, if only for a short time, it's there. I need this.

ASH. Then I could be anyone.

LAILA. Just anyone? No.

ASH (*childishly*). Why me?

LAILA. Because you're willing to take this risk too. (*Ash is uneasy.*) I know you don't like to think about it . . . but it's there. You're just as guilty, if ever found out. So I could ask you the same question. Why do it, Ash?

ASH. I like you. I like this. That's it.

LAILA. If you like "this," get married.

ASH. Why?

LAILA. Your life would be easier.

ASH. Not here.

LAILA. You want a life you can't have.

ASH. Why can't I?

LAILA. Born in the wrong place at the wrong time.

ASH. You make it sound hopeless.

LAILA. Not for you but for me, probably.

ASH. You could go out.

LAILA. Covered from head to toe, with a slit in the middle of my face to see where I'm going? Accompanied by some teenage nephew who's fifteen years younger than myself—who knows only this—this—which tells him that he has power over me, despite age and experience, power because of his gender. So we go out—but where? To do what?

ASH. So you do this?

LAILA. I don't mind. Do you?

ASH. Obviously not.

LAILA. It's funny . . . taking money for sex is my humanity . . . my slight attempt of holding on to whatever life I had in the past. But in my past, I never would have even thought of doing this. Isn't that funny?

ASH. No.

LAILA. Yes.

ASH. What?

LAILA. I like you. I like you and I like to eat and have heat and hot water. Can't I like it all?

Ash pulls Laila closer to him.

ASH. Yes.

LAILA. I think other women do . . . this. Don't worry. It's something never spoken of, left unsaid. Not all of us widows, but there are some, I know.

ASH. I guess there are few alternatives.

LAILA. None. Well, except one. (*Both are silent for a while.*) You know what I mean?

ASH. I don't want to think about that.

LAILA. But death's everywhere.

ASH. Not in this bed.

LAILA (*coming closer to Ash*). No, not here.

ASH. Why doesn't your family help you more?

LAILA. There's nothing to give except our male relatives who can accompany me when I need to go out. That's about all they can do for me. I'll take it, though. Those are the only times I can leave. If someone can't take me out, I feel like . . . I could go crazy, you know? Even though everything's so blurred out there. I can't see very clearly under my burqa, but I'm outside, under the sun. Though I really have trouble seeing it, I can feel it. It's salvation, for a moment.

ASH. They don't know how you live?

LAILA. They would kill me. You know that.

ASH. Maybe not.

LAILA. It wasn't hard, doing this with men who weren't my husband.

ASH. Why?

LAILA. Because I always liked being with him. I think more than he liked being with me. I enjoyed it.

ASH. More than you enjoyed him?

LAILA. Isn't it one and the same?

ASH. I don't know.

LAILA. And I enjoy you.

ASH. I didn't ask.

LAILA. But you wanted to know.

ASH. Why only me, now? You could have more money if you had others.

LAILA. I don't want others. It started out as a necessity. Necessity to have a connection, a physical connection with another being. Then it was necessary to have food and heat and hot water . . . and now, it's necessity . . . to be . . . wanted . . . by just one other person.

ASH. That's not much to ask for.

LAILA. What else can I ask for? (*Gets up from her bed to paint.*)

Ash pulls on his trousers and follows her.

ASH. If you were allowed to remarry . . .

LAILA. I'm not.

ASH. But if you were . . .

LAILA. I would never expect anything from you.

ASH. Why?

LAILA. Because this is all we're meant to be. Afternoons, waiting for you, making love to you, taking your money, and painting my windows black! That's all this is. It will never be more than this moment!

ASH. I want more.

LAILA. I think you should have more. I think you should find someone to marry.

ASH. I have.

LAILA. How could you possibly know? From our times in that bed? Because that's all we've had.

ASH (*angry*). It's more than what the others have had! (*Crosses to the chair at downstage right and puts on clothes.*) You probably didn't even know your husband when you married him!

LAILA. You're right! I didn't. But that's what was normal, and this isn't.

ASH. Who says so?

LAILA. I do! Look at me! With this fucking paintbrush in my hand, painting the fucking windows black! Is this normal? Is this something you do at home? No, because you're not a widow! You're not a woman! Is it normal for me, for me, for who I was, to take money from you and other men for having sex with them, so I could feel another human being next to me and not starve at the same time? Is that normal? No, it's not. But wait—in another way it is, because it's what's normal now. It's the new normal. The normal that can't see if it's day or night! The normal that makes your windows black and asks a teenage boy to take you out into the street because you can't go by yourself. The new normal that takes your work from you, the work you did before this, so now you're made to do . . . this. For the child I buried, this would have been her normal, without ever knowing anything different. I'm glad she doesn't have to know "this." (*Breaks down, throws the paintbrush to the floor. Ash puts his arms around her, drawing her closer.*) She was sick. It was after my husband died. And I couldn't find any male relative to take us out—but out where? We could only see a female physician, and there were none anymore. But I thought someone, a male doctor, who would understand, who would have sympathy, or regret, would see us. So I just took her myself. That was the first time I had ever broken the law. They immediately arrested me. I got beaten up. No doctor saw her anyway. I guess it was for nothing. She was gone. And then, after that day, I was gone. Except, I'm still here.

ASH. I wish . . .

LAILA. So do I. (*Picks up a brush and resumes painting.*) I wish too.

ASH. This place is freezing. (*Returns to the chair and continues dressing.*)

LAILA. Is it? I wouldn't know.

ASH. I hate saying this . . . but I think you need to see others . . . you need more . . . to survive.

LAILA. Do I? I thought I was fine.

ASH. You're not.

LAILA. Should I be?

Beat.

ASH. No.

LAILA. Then this is sufficient, right?

ASH. Can I help you?

LAILA. No. It's my job now. (*Ash turns away, finishes dressing, and puts on his boots.*) Why aren't you married?

ASH. I don't want to be, at least not here. Not like this.

LAILA. What if it'll always be like this?

ASH. Then I'll never marry.

LAILA. What do you do? I never asked. Those kinds of questions don't mean anything anymore. So I never bothered.

ASH. So why bother now?

LAILA (*comes centerstage*). Because we like each other. And I suppose that's what people who like each other ask. Questions like those, normal questions, about normal life.

ASH. And you ask me these normal questions about a normal life as you blacken your windows.

LAILA. It's funny, right? Everything's becoming funny here, isn't it?

ASH. No, it's not.

LAILA. Well, if I can laugh, so should you.

ASH. I don't want to.

LAILA. Why are you so serious now?

ASH. I'm not.

LAILA. Did my normal question offend you?

ASH. I'm not offended.

LAILA (*sits on chair at stage left and poses formally*). I was an English teacher. I graduated from university and everything. I taught in secondary school—boys and girls. Can you believe that? I even taught with other men. The head teacher was a woman. Isn't that funny?

ASH (*uncomfortable*). No, it's not.

LAILA. I told you. Now you could tell me. See, I made it easy for you, didn't I?

ASH (*throws money on the bed*). That should be enough.

LAILA. I even told you about her and how she died!

ASH (*moves toward the door*). I have to go.

LAILA. But I have another funny thing to tell you!

ASH. I'm not interested.

LAILA. I know what you do! (*Ash takes off hat and scarf and turns slowly.*) I saw you. At the football stadium. I walked past . . . my nephew wanted to see! He heard the screams and it excited him! He wanted to see! I didn't. I never would have. He dragged me . . . he pulled my arm . . . he was moving so fast that there were times my feet were off the ground . . . I even fell down once. But he wanted to see! So we saw! We saw the executions . . . of people like me . . . people . . . like all of us! For nothing! And then we saw you! I saw you! I saw you in your uniform that made you look so stupid and so arrogant! Your religious police uniform! Do you know how that sounds? I saw you! You never turned away. You never winced . . . you never moved . . . you were just so still. It never bothered you.

ASH. It did! It does!

LAILA (*runs around the bed*). You're going to kill me, in there, with the others! That's why you're here!

ASH. I'm not! (*Catching Laila and putting his arms around her shoulders.*) I'm helping you!

LAILA (*pulling away*). How?

ASH. I keep them away! They don't know. I make sure this address is never on their list.

LAILA. Their list?

ASH. Of places to search.

LAILA. For what?

ASH. Anything.

LAILA. Anything that doesn't "fit" with this new place that we've found ourselves in.

ASH. I guess. I don't know. I never ask.

LAILA. No. Someone like you would never ask.

ASH (*in a guilty voice*). It's just like what you're doing!

LAILA (*stands on the bed and throws pillows at Ash*). I don't hang people in a football stadium.

ASH (*desperately searching*). It's . . . just . . . as morally wrong!

LAILA (*quietly*). If you believe it's the same wrong, you're just like them. (*Ash tries to grab Laila. Falls on to the bed and cries. Laila continues, in a reflective mood.*) But I don't think you're like them. They've *made* us like that, and yes we can be made to do things. (*Stroking his body as he cries*) I never believed that before. I never thought anyone could make you do anything. I remember at school once, I was scolded by the teacher for laughing. And I told the teacher that this boy behind me was saying these funny things, and making me laugh. And she said nobody could make me do anything. I chose to laugh. Is that the same as my choosing to work in this bed and your choosing to work in that football stadium? Some people may say so. I'm still angry at you now, for doing that. Because I can't understand how loving you could be here with me, as opposed to how brutal you could be outside with them. But maybe we could become different people. Maybe we could actually be made to change, to do things we never would have done. To not know if it's day or night. To paint our windows black. Maybe we could be made to do anything, and think it's all right. You don't have to come back again. (*Stands and walks to the chair at downstage left.*)

ASH. But I want to. (*Crosses to Laila.*) Please . . . I swear to you! You could believe me! No one would have to know! I'd be punished just the same! So why would I take that risk?

LAILA. Why would you?

ASH (*desperately*). I wouldn't. I want you. And I want to help you, so if this helps, let me come back.

LAILA. Maybe I don't want you to.

ASH. But you need me.

LAILA. I need my husband back. I need my daughter back. I need my teaching back. I need to go outside again by myself, and not worry about getting arrested for it. I need to be allowed to see my arms and legs when I walk outside. I need to see my face in a window's reflection. I need the sunlight to come through my windows. You see, I need a lot of things, I don't have. What's one more? (*Beat. Ash takes his jacket from the bed and puts it on. He moves to the door, opens the door, and waits.*) You'd better hurry. You wouldn't want to be seen.

Ash chooses to leave and swiftly exits. Laila takes her paintbrush. Then stops and throws the brush on the floor. Goes to her bed, takes a sheet, takes a bottle of water from the floor and proceeds to clean the blackened window to reveal the sunlight. She removes the paint with all her might. Thene takes off her slip and stands naked at the window.

Lights dim.

PART 3. Kabul

Kabul. Winter, 2005. A bombed apartment. The stage is stark with two chairs facing the audience on the apron stage in front of a curtain. Ash occupies one chair. He has aged and appears very disconcerted.

ASH. What do I remember? I remember . . . black. Black walls . . . no light . . . no sunlight. Nothing to tell me if it was day or night. I had seen that darkness once before. So that stays with me . . . that feeling . . . that lack of . . . everything but that feeling. Dates . . . times . . . are very distant from me. I apologize if I can't be clearer for you, but I can't. Everything is very far away, except that darkness. It's like a dream . . . but not a good one . . . so you don't want to remember it, even though you're told you should remember it. You tell yourself and others tell it to you. But why try? What would matter now? It's already happened . . . that very dreamlike strange time in that very brutally strange place. I'm not sure what I said before. I can't be certain . . . but I am certain of her. She was there, with me. You see, I put her there. Different hands controlled the puppet strings, but it was the same place and the same feeling, and that same brutality. Mine came from . . . them, and hers came from me. I was part of the . . . whole . . . what do we call it now? Regime? Event? Whatever that was . . . that kept her hidden . . . silenced . . . restrained. And now I was too. I kept thinking, "This is what she knew. This was her entire being. This is what she felt, and now I feel it too. She got me back." My payback. But the really bizarre thing was that I was imprisoned all those months for the wrong reason, I think. I don't think they knew about . . . her . . . or truly understood what I had done to her, and to others like her, maybe like you. So it's a bit funny now isn't it? All for the wrong reason. I thought I was right, maybe, or maybe . . . it was all I knew, really knew. So how could it be wrong, if no one told me it was. I don't justify my actions, but I know that's how it sounds, doesn't it? What am I trying to tell you . . . I was . . . the police . . . the religious police . . . I thought I was good and moral and right. No, wait. I don't think I ever did . . . because I found her and let her in. She was a widow, who taught me the English I speak to you today. Who taught me how to blacken windows so no one knew if it was day or night. She was the one I saved and killed at the same time. I never put a rope around anyone's neck . . . I promise you, I never did that. But what I did to her was worse than that, because I led her to feel that having that rope put around her neck in the football stadium would have been better . . . than this.

Lights up on Dahlia, wearing a hijab, seated in the other chair. Ash is seated at stage left, smoking continuously. Dahlia, seated on chair at stage right, takes notes. They never face each other during their interview.

DAHLIA. Maybe it was.

ASH. Maybe she was right, in the end.

DAHLIA. Do you want to stop?

ASH. Why are you interviewing me?

DAHLIA. You should be heard.

ASH. But you're not telling my story. Your work is supposedly about women and war, women who lived in this place . . . during . . . that time.

DAHLIA. We have trouble identifying exactly what "that time" should be called.

ASH. So why interview me?

DAHLIA. If she were here, I'd speak to her and to the others like her, but they're not. You're the closest I have to them.

ASH. I wonder what you see right now.

DAHLIA (*uneasy*). I don't agree . . . support . . . torture. If that's what you're wondering. I suppose if you really were such a threat, you wouldn't be here, outside, here, free, to speak with me, to stay, to go. I suppose that's what they realized, though it took several months to come to that realization.

ASH. That's not what I wonder. I don't give a shit about your views on torture, or politics, or war, or any other fucking thing.

DAHLIA. I know what you wonder.

ASH. So tell me.

DAHLIA. It doesn't matter what I think.

ASH. I'm giving you my time . . . my words . . . so the least you can do is give me what's inside your head.

DAHLIA. She taught you well.

ASH. I never needed a translator.

DAHLIA. Congratulations.

ASH. It made me better off than most.

DAHLIA. If that's possible.

ASH. It was. (*Beat.*) You despise me.

DAHLIA. I don't know you well enough to.

ASH. Is that an offer?

DAHLIA. She did this to you.

ASH. What?

DAHLIA. She made you feel and laugh even at something like this, now. She gave you . . . joy.

ASH. Is that what this is?

DAHLIA. I don't know, but it's something.

ASH. But she didn't have any to give.

DAHLIA. That's what I wonder, about her and others like her. Was it possible to still . . . love . . . under such restrictions, and allow yourself to be loved?

ASH. You could answer that. You know war.

DAHLIA. Not behind burqas or blackened windows.

ASH. Did you love?

DAHLIA. It wasn't the same.

ASH. Did you?

DAHLIA. Yes. But not enough.

ASH. I loved her.

DAHLIA. But not enough.

ASH (*reflective*). No.

DAHLIA. Could you have saved her, when she was found out for whatever moral crime she had committed?

ASH. I could have tried.

DAHLIA. You knew what would happen to her?

ASH. Yes.

DAHLIA. Though you did nothing to stop it.

ASH. Not enough.

DAHLIA. You must have been scared.

ASH. More justification. You're too kind.

DAHLIA. I'm trying to understand.

ASH. I don't think we ever will. I don't think we can.

DAHLIA. You are different.

ASH. I'm the nice fundamentalist.

DAHLIA. That's not what I meant.

ASH. You want to attribute everything to her . . . Laila.

DAHLIA. That was her name? It sounds like mine.

ASH. You want to give her the credit for making me different. Love, but not enough, protect, but not enough, feel, but not enough.

DAHLIA. If it weren't for her, you would never have been able to speak to me like this.

ASH. And so I can. So now what?

DAHLIA. She pierced you.

ASH. And what did I give her in return? Nothing.

DAHLIA. Companionship? Friendship? I wasn't there. Only you would know.

ASH. I gave her . . . the absolute power to give up. That deep dark sinking pit that tells you it's over. You've lost, so let it be done with as quickly as possible. That's your dignity, the only piece you have left, because you decided when it would happen, rather than lose sleep and breath waiting for it. You've told it when to come for you.

DAHLIA. It was her doing . . . to give up.

ASH. I was the catalyst.

DAHLIA. So you're a believer in collective responsibility, then?

ASH. Whatever that is . . . whatever that does. I think there was so little left to believe in . . . when she found out about me and what I did, that was it.

DAHLIA. I think it was possible for her . . . to feel something, to love, even under this . . . vacuum of any emotion or thought.

ASH. You couldn't have?

DAHLIA. I'm writing about these women, not myself.

ASH. You're so separate from them? Isn't it the same? Women? War? Religion? All that?

DAHLIA. It isn't.

ASH. So she's the better person. Better than me . . . better than you. She wins. And we're left, here. Good for her! Maybe I did her a favor.

DAHLIA. Maybe you'll find someone else . . . someone like Laila.

ASH. Never. There was no one before Laila and the possibility of there being one now, doesn't exist. I'm stripped, you see. A shell. You think there's something more, something left. There isn't. I have nothing to give. I don't even know if I want to give to anyone, or let anyone in. You're the first person I've spoken to like this, since her. I don't know why, but I let you be here and listen to me. I don't know why. She left with her dignity. I have none, because of what put me in prison and because of what happened once I was imprisoned. So, she is the winner.

DAHLIA. Yes, your story is very sad. But you can't call her a winner! Look at the life she and the others had! Look at how she died! You say it was with dignity? But how could something so horrible and so public for something so fucking bizarre and incomprehensibly illegal be dignified? It can't.

ASH. You sit in front of me and look at me with my head lowered to see if I've learned some lesson, don't you? You think, "He has no right to have an opinion, to say it aloud. He should be meek and sorry. He's not sorry enough. He thinks he is, but it's not enough. He says he's a shell, but he should be less than that. There's too much here. Oh he looks bad and old and a bit confused, without much to look forward to, but it should be worse." Even though you say how you don't agree with this or that, you still see me as your enemy.

DAHLIA. You can't make that judgment.

ASH. I can! I've spent enough time watching people watch me, waiting for me to say what they want me to say. I know what they think.

DAHLIA. You can't place me with your interrogators.

ASH. That's where you are now. The only difference is that I've accepted your invitation.

DAHLIA. Why?

ASH. Because it's all I know now. Maybe it's all I've ever known. Maybe I never had a mind of my own and that's what led me to this moment. Perhaps that's why I was able to follow, without protest, and do what I did and not think it wrong, until someone without fear told me, yes, it was wrong. Maybe that's why I've let you in.

DAHLIA. And if she hadn't told you different, you would never have thought . . .

ASH. Thought?

DAHLIA. Felt. (*Beat.*) I think I wanted to despise you.

ASH. It would have given you something to feel.

DAHLIA. Why did you just say that?

ASH. You didn't need torture to become . . . this . . . like me.

DAHLIA. I am not like you.

ASH. Without . . . I'm left without her, and you're without . . . something . . . someone. That's what drives you to do this, relieve pain. You want to find something that will make you . . . come alive again.

DAHLIA. I thought I was, with, not devoid of feeling, or life, or . . . joy.

ASH. I'm sorry. I don't know you. I don't know anyone anymore. It's not my right to say those things, I suppose.

Dahlia collects her bag and notes.

DAHLIA. I'm truly sorry for you, for what you've been through. It was . . . a terrible . . . shame.

ASH. For you too.

DAHLIA. Despite what you were before this . . . I don't think she— Laila—would have wanted you to go through what you did.

ASH. Me? Before this? What exactly was before this? Aren't I the same person? I can't remember anything . . . good. Not anything. In my recollection, my earliest recollection, there were always football stadiums to hang people, and very heavy veils, and blackened windows . . . things like that, blocks, obstacles, that never allowed us to see . . . the other. To see . . . you. To look at Laila and see what she was thinking or feeling. There was always this very high wall separating us . . . men from women . . . boys from girls. Growing up, I couldn't climb over and get past that wall, though I was curious. Would the world on the other side of that wall be . . . bad, wrong, some place I shouldn't know? I always wondered, wondered if I were to see, to finally see, would it change me? Would it . . . touch me? Leave me . . . different? But one day, I found Laila, and I did manage to get past that wall. And that world on the other side wasn't an evil place, not for me. I did see her. She did touch me. And that changed me.

DAHLIA (*refers to her notes*). Now I don't know what I should do with all this. This was all on my own. I don't have a publisher yet. But, now I don't know what to do. It's very unclear to me.

ASH. What you intended to do. Write about her. Write about them.

DAHLIA. And you, now.

ASH. Not me. She's the one who needs to be remembered. I don't want to be.

DAHLIA. Of course not by name. I would maintain your privacy . . .

ASH. Why would I need to be included? I was a small person in this entire . . . mess . . . that you like to call it. I was . . . no one, you see.

DAHLIA. I don't know what I see, anymore.

ASH. So you've caught what I have. It's very . . . unclear. Except, I see how much we stay the same. Our interrogators' names change, but the questions . . . are all the same.

DAHLIA. I wish I could have spoken to her.

ASH. Then she would have been like anyone else.

DAHLIA. Why do we think death makes us greater?

ASH. Because it does.

DAHLIA. That's frightening.

ASH. That's all there's left.

DAHLIA. Then what was everything for?

ASH. I was hoping you could tell me, because I'm having a very hard time trying to understand this myself.

DAHLIA. It led you to her, to knowing her, in the way you did.

ASH. Then I think the price was too great.

DAHLIA. Do you start again?

ASH. From where? Here?

DAHLIA. It could be better.

ASH. Not for a very long time. That's what people don't understand.

DAHLIA (*crosses upstage of her chair*). Thank you for your help . . . for your time . . . your words.

ASH. Whatever you do with them, know that I am sorry, for my silence in hurting her.

Dahlia starts to leave.

DAHLIA. She surrendered . . . everything. That's all she did.

ASH. Not in despair.

DAHLIA. No. Not in despair.

Dahlia exits stage right.

Lights dim on Ash.

PART 4.New York

New York. Spring, 2005. An apartment bedroom. Late night. Susan tries to sleep. Restless, she gets out of bed, puts on a robe, sits at the foot of the bed.

SUSAN (*to the audience*). I was a spectacle. That's how he first saw me . . . as a spectacle. Twenty-five years ago, on campus, our junior year at Tulane, Peter first saw me as a spectacle, lying bloodied in the middle of the road, after having been hit by a car that came out of absolutely . . . nowhere. It was early autumn, October 18th. Everyone was rushing to . . . somewhere. I suppose I had been also, though I can't remember where. Maybe it was to meet someone, though I never showed. I never asked where he was going or where he had been. Or if there was someone waiting for him, and who it was, and was it important, and would that person forgive him for never showing. I never asked him any of that. All I remember was being hit from behind and tossed into the air, only to fall and roll, at an incredible speed, like a scene you fast forward, aware of everything staying still as I rolled past it all . . . gravel and concrete and broken bottles and cigarette butts and cars tires and people's shoes and dog shit. I saw it all on that very bizarre roller coaster, until, I came to a stop. And then, I, panting, scared, feeling as if I were about to die, if I weren't already dead . . . was still. And from the ground, I saw the sky. It had been blue but had turned gray, and a bit dead, like autumn. I was conscious . . . I suppose. Aware, but uncertain . . . uncertain that I was still . . . here. Though I must have been terribly aware, because I began to feel like a spectacle, a show, that any passerby wanted to stop for and see. I'm not exactly sure what they wanted to see. But that's how I remember Peter, as one of those spectators, albeit a genuine one. One who truly cared for . . . a stranger. There were thousands of students on campus. I hadn't seen him before. He was a journalism major, and I . . . wasn't. He would never have known someone like me. I had no desire to go anywhere, and he wanted to go . . . everywhere. I pretended I knew nothing, and he made me believe he knew . . . everything. He came to me, kneeled beside me, held my hand and told me that I was alive, that everything would be fine. I wanted to get up and run away, from the accident, from the people, from my blood, from myself, but he told me I shouldn't move, I was alive. Hearing it from him . . . this genuinely good spectator, made me believe that I indeed was alive, and yes, that everything would be fine. Is that what he still is? What he's always been? A spectator? Is that why he'll go . . . anywhere . . . anywhere threatening? Is that why he stayed with me throughout the accident, that evening, and twenty-five years on? Maybe it's because he couldn't let go of my hand. I thought it was I . . . the weaker one, or so I always thought, the one less honored, that it was I who couldn't or wouldn't let go. But perhaps I've been mistaken all this time. Maybe I can. Maybe I always could. He stays with them, the spectacles from the car accidents, later to become the car bombs and gunfire and landmines. He holds their bloodied hands under a dead autumn sky and assures them they too will be fine. He stays with them until they truly will be, or at least they believe they will be fine. They believe he'll stay forever. But he can't, because there'll always be the next spectacle he has to run to and observe and report on and reassure. He'll make it OK for them, for that moment. Rwanda. Afghanistan. Sarajevo . . . for all of them. He'll save them, with his words, his being, at that moment, because they need to be saved . . . by him, return to me, feel home again, and then . . . start out again. Unfortunately, for him, it's become very . . . familiar . . . very still . . . not the politics, not a war, or a conflict, but something else . . . something deeper . . . more profound . . . that's made him . . . question himself and his role as savior. If his role has been questioned, then mine has too. Because I had always been the reason to return. I, being the familiar. The privilege of being his very first spectacle! What are we now? Am I to be the one to release his hand first and tell him everything will be okay? He may listen, but not respond. He's silent now. He looks at me with nothing to say. Silence is also abusive. Having someone look at you and be . . . regretful for having made . . . the safer choice . . . the easier-to-explain choice. You're easier to explain because you have no history of your own. He is your past and your present. Silence is abuse when you realize he has nothing to say to you. And that whatever your voice is struggling to say is . . . meaningless . . . valueless . . . nothing. Silence. Like the silence in your head when you've been thrown onto the pavement on a Fall morning and every breath, word, thought, feeling has been knocked out of you, so in that moment you are . . . nothing. And now that moment has become this moment. That silence in my head those years past are his silence very present and very real.

Lights dim.

PART 5. Dubrovnik

Dubrovnik. Summer, 2006. A seaside hotel room. The stage is brightly lit. There is an ornate desk by the window and two chairs downstage, left and right respectively. Tony enters from the shower, naked, wiping himself with his towel. He crosses to the window, puts the towel around his waist, picks up a book with Dahlia's picture on the back cover. Dahlia enters from the shower, her hair in a towel. Her robe is open. She too is naked underneath.

TONY (*looks at the picture, then looks at Dahlia*). You look different.

DAHLIA. How?

TONY. Your hair, up like that. It makes you look . . . vulnerable.

DAHLIA. You mean, younger?

TONY. No. Just vulnerable. (*Dahlia closes her robe.*) You don't like that?

DAHLIA (*sits on chair at downstage right*). No. Do you want me to be vulnerable?

TONY. It's sweet, sometimes.

DAHLIA. So you want me to be sweet now?

TONY. You already are.

DAHLIA. No, I'm not.

TONY. Okay, so you're not, then. (*Moves centerstage, takes his robe off, and holds it like a bullfighter's cape. Dahlia discards her towel and poses like a bull. She charges at the towel, landing on the bed. They jump on the bed, roll on and under the sheets, creating strange shapes under them. Dahlia's head pops out at stage left, left of the bed. Tony kisses her passionately.*)

DAHLIA. I hope I'm not mistaken.

TONY. Why would you be?

DAHLIA. This. I never anticipated . . . this.

TONY. And I did?

DAHLIA. I don't know, Tony.

TONY. I didn't. You're funny.

DAHLIA. Never heard that one said to me before.

TONY. You're waiting for something bad to happen.

DAHLIA. Why would you say that?

TONY. You're waiting for me to be an asshole, so you could say, "See. I knew he was just like the others."

DAHLIA. No, I'm not. Are you?

TONY. What?

DAHLIA. An asshole?

Tony plays under the covers.

TONY (*laughing*). I knew it! I knew it! I was waiting for it. (*They continue to be playful and physical.*) What do you think?

DAHLIA. I don't know.

TONY. You don't?

DAHLIA. No.

TONY. All right, then. Believe what you wish.

DAHLIA (*moves closer to kiss Tony*). I will.

They kiss.

TONY. These days, have been . . . really nice.

DAHLIA. A very unexpected . . . surprise.

TONY. That's what surprises are.

DAHLIA. Are they? I wouldn't know.

TONY. I doubt that. I bet you've been adorned with surprises, a lot nicer than a weekend in Dubrovnik.

DAHLIA. Not true.

TONY. Why then?

DAHLIA. I don't know.

TONY. Really?

DAHLIA. If I did, I'd tell you.

TONY. Maybe it's what we do, as writers and journalists and humanitarians and peacekeepers, though paradoxical the latter sounds as there's actually very little peace in our history. We don't want to be in one place long enough for anything . . .

Dahlia kisses Tony.

DAHLIA. More than a weekend in Dubrovnik in a hotel room, by the sea?

TONY. I didn't say that.

DAHLIA. But I did. I can't seem to get myself out of hotel rooms. It's like they've become attached to myself or something.

TONY. That's . . . appealing. (*Moves in to kiss Dahlia.*)

DAHLIA (*turns away*). But I don't want that anymore.

TONY (*sits up*). Why have it in the first place?

DAHLIA (*sits up in bed*). I could ask you the same question. Who is your home?

TONY. I never wanted anyone to be my home. That's the truth. But it's not your truth.

DAHLIA. It's out of my control. Everything is.

TONY. That's a clever bulletproof vest to wear.

DAHLIA. Yeah, I don't know why it's been the way it's been. So I'll wear it for as long as I can.

TONY. Not forever.

DAHLIA. It's been longer than I thought.

TONY. If that's the way you want it to be.

DAHLIA. So it's my fault? My choices?

TONY. As one of your present choices, I'll keep my mouth shut on that one.

DAHLIA. You started.

TONY. Like a child. "You started."

DAHLIA *(playful)*. You approached me first.

TONY. And you responded.

DAHLIA. But you were first.

A pillow fight begins.

TONY. You're right then, I started.

DAHLIA. See? *(Takes off her robe.)*

TONY. I see.

DAHLIA. Why did you come?

Playfulness stops.

TONY. Are you sorry?

DAHLIA. Not at all.

TONY. Well, I finished my article earlier than anticipated . . . there was nothing assigned to me at the moment, so I just thought, "why not?"

DAHLIA. Why not call first?

TONY. I don't know why. I just took the chance. If you were busy, you had plans, fine. I'd have a weekend in Dubrovnik on my own. If you were free, well, that would be fine too. I only hope I didn't take you away from anything.

DAHLIA. No. It was the perfect time. The conference had already ended, I had booked a few extra days. It was . . . perfect timing.

TONY. I'm glad, then. I wouldn't want to intrude.

DAHLIA. You didn't. I'm happy you're here.

TONY. It worked out.

DAHLIA. I'm sorry you missed the conference.

TONY. I would have liked to have heard you speak . . . about . . . what was the topic again?

DAHLIA. Documenting trauma.

TONY. Ugh! Then again . . .

DAHLIA. It wasn't that heavy.

TONY. I doubt that.

DAHLIA. I'm sure you could say something about that.

TONY. I'm sure I could. We all have our stories.

DAHLIA. But you've never written about yourself.

TONY. Maybe I don't find myself that interesting. Maybe I'd rather write about someone else.

DAHLIA. It's easier than writing about yourself.

TONY. You'd understand that as well I. (*Dahlia frees herself from Tony's grip, goes over to the desk overlooking the sea, pours a drink, and picks up the book. Tony slides to the foot of the bed and sits on its edge*) I re-read it.

DAHLIA. When?

TONY. Last night. While you were asleep. It touched me.

DAHLIA. Did it? Who was more sympathetic?

TONY. They're both pathetic.

DAHLIA. Pathetic?

TONY. How else would you define their existence? I wouldn't even say they had a chance to have an existence. You said it yourself. We have very little control. And your Ash and Laila in your story had far less than that.

DAHLIA. What's the point then? Why would they have even attempted to be . . . normal, and have a . . . normal existence?

TONY. Because it's a story, whether it be truth or fiction. That's what all stories want, even the fantastical ones, an element of normalcy. That's what you're hoping for, isn't it? And there's nothing wrong with that, Dahlia. Nothing at all. Even I've come to that realization. Just now. That's why this time is so

. . . nice, because it's so . . . normal. We meet. We get along. It's not too heavy. We don't ask for the names of our pasts. We walk around the city like a . . . normal couple, and take photos of ourselves and ask others to take our picture together, so we could be like . . . them. We eat. We drink. We laugh. We make love. It's easy, you see? That's what your couple in your story wanted. They just wanted to be normal, to be like other people. But they couldn't. That's what makes them . . . sad.

DAHLIA. They had no hope.

TONY. Not in their skin . . . in their existence. No.

DAHLIA. Why even try?

TONY. Because they're human. Taking that risk, kept them . . . alive.

DAHLIA. It killed Laila in the end.

TONY. On her terms . . . I think. Perhaps I misunderstood . . .

DAHLIA. No. You read it right. (*Sits at the foot of the bed with Tony and finishes her drink.*) We collect people. We can't help it. We can't disregard them, so they become a part of us. She's a part of me now. So is he.

TONY. Does everyone from your past have a piece of you?

DAHLIA. I hope not.

TONY. Why?

DAHLIA. It would be a pull . . . and it'd hold me back.

TONY. Some people have a stronger pull than others. You're one of them. On me.

DAHLIA. I'm sorry.

TONY. Why?

DAHLIA. It's not what you expected . . . what you want.

TONY. What I've wanted. Things change . . . people change.

DAHLIA. No, we don't. We never change.

TONY. That's depressing.

DAHLIA. Why do you want to change?

TONY. Not really change, but be . . . more. More than I am. Than I was yesterday. More than I was before knowing you. (*Takes her hand.*)

DAHLIA. Do you think everyone thinks that way, about everyone they meet?

TONY. Are you talking about him?

DAHLIA. Who?

TONY (*moves to the head of the bed*). An unnamed piece of your past you collected along the way? Are you wondering if knowing you made him better?

DAHLIA. I don't care.

TONY. Some pulls are stronger than others.

DAHLIA. It obviously was nothing.

TONY. It's never nothing. I'm sure he's regretful.

DAHLIA. I doubt it.

TONY. Not everyone's life is better than your own. (*Beat.*) Do you want him back?

DAHLIA. I never had him in the first place.

TONY. That's worse, then. Never having, makes you wonder, what could have been.

DAHLIA. But I'm tired of playing "what if's." It's taken too much away. Too many missed opportunities, some I never even saw.

TONY. So now you know better.

DAHLIA. I hope so.

TONY. I hope so too.

> *Dahlia and Tony move closer to each other.*
> *Lights dim.*

YASMINE BEVERLY RANA

New York. Spring 2007. Sidewalk in front of a bookstore. An easel bears a sign announcing a book reading. Dahlia reads to the audience. We hear her but do not see her. Peter enters with an umbrella. It is raining.

DAHLIA. "She pierced him. She pierced him in a place very far away from anything . . . normal. But what about him? Him before her? What exactly was before her? They were both . . . without. He was left without her, and she . . . needed something or someone to make her . . . come alive again. She wasn't quite dead, just . . . un-alive. For then. For that moment. But not forever."

Peter hears her reading and the subsequent applause. Lights up. Dahlia enters from stage left, opens her umbrella, and tries to hail a taxi. It is raining. She doesn't notice Peter who approaches her. Peter is older, more tired, and "less alive."

PETER. I thought your book was beautiful.

DAHLIA (*surprised, but not completely*). You're here! Did you read it? All of it?

PETER. Every word.

DAHLIA. Thank you.

PETER. (*Beat.*) Was she, you?

DAHLIA (*astonished*). Who?

PETER. The woman in your book. Laila. I know it's fiction, and she's from Afghanistan, and you're not. But there's always that element of truth, so I was just wondering.

DAHLIA (*uneasy*). Why did you just say that?

PETER. I'm sorry. I didn't mean to offend you.

DAHLIA (*shaken*). I don't know how you could come to that conclusion.

PETER. I just saw you . . . strength . . . love . . . the ability to continue to love, even in a very cruel place. Maybe it wasn't about Laila, but I guess I still . . . occasionally . . . have trouble keeping away from you, even when you're very far away, even now, after so much time.

DAHLIA (*adamant*). But Laila died. (*Attempts to hail a taxi.*)

PETER. I know. So did I . . . to you.

DAHLIA. I said that, didn't I? It's strange what we come up with when we're threatened.

PETER. Did I threaten you?

DAHLIA. Not you. Well, maybe. But I don't think it was intentional. We say things we don't mean under fire, or when we're coerced to say it. I've learned that because of this book.

PETER. So I coerced you?

DAHLIA. You were bringing attention. (*Crosses to stage right, still searching for a taxi and trying to avoid Peter.*)

PETER. As you're doing now.

DAHLIA. You still believe that?

PETER. Yes. Don't you?

DAHLIA. No. No, I don't. I've become . . . you.

PETER. I don't understand.

DAHLIA. You wouldn't. How could you? But I can. Because I was Laila and her executioner and the other women and my translators! And when I was them, in Sarajevo, I spoke to you because I thought I had to. Because I thought at that moment you had the power I could never . . . possibly would never have.

PETER. You offered, Dahlia. I never forced you to give me your story. You wanted me to hear it.

DAHLIA. We very charmingly persuade them, Peter.

PETER. Journalists brought the world to Sarajevo and made it listen!

DAHLIA. We left! You left Sarajevo! I left Kabul! Kabul gave me this moment as Sarajevo gave you yours! We're ungrateful guests.

PETER. How much money are you making off your host?

DAHLIA. More than I ever had or could ever imagine having. And that's why I hate myself. Did you also hate yourself, Peter?

PETER. I had no reason to.

DAHLIA. I wish I could be more like you and be able to say that and actually believe that, if you indeed believe you're blameless.

PETER. Not completely blameless, but accepting.

DAHLIA. Of what?

PETER. Of this being the way it is.

DAHLIA. I can't accept it.

PETER. Then stop. Stop writing. Stop asking. Stop listening. Give it all up.

DAHLIA. You don't understand. I hate myself because I don't want to. I don't want to stop. It's not just the money, but this—speaking and having the power to be heard, to be asked what I think. To . . . coerce my . . . subjects to let me speak for them, to be their voice. You see, I've become a bit of an addict. I want the next level and I'll go wherever I have to . . . to reach that. How far did you go?

PETER. As far as I could.

DAHLIA. With no regrets?

PETER. I don't think about that, Dahlia.

DAHLIA. Right. Because it's the end result that's important, taking the world to its knees to see . . . hell. To convey what it sounds like, looks like, feels like . . . Nothing else matters, right?

PETER. It's exactly like that.

Beat. Sound of rain and car horns.

DAHLIA. Did you ever return to Sarajevo?

PETER. You would have known if I had.

DAHLIA. Perhaps not.

PETER. Why wouldn't I have contacted you?

DAHLIA. Was mine the only story you heard? (*Peter is unable to answer*.) No. I didn't think it was. Now, I can see it wasn't, and I wouldn't have expected it to be.

PETER. Dahlia, my intentions were honorable. I never used anyone.

DAHLIA. Intentions usually are honorable. It's what follows that becomes flawed and mistaken.

PETER. No, I never returned.

DAHLIA. And I haven't returned to Kabul. Why should I? Why should you have returned to Sarajevo or any of the other places you honorably used for your career? Your book was written, as mine is. We don't need them anymore. My translators . . . the women I met . . . even their executioners . . . they trusted me. They let me inside. I put them at risk under that obscure umbrella of truth . . . and then I abandoned them. (*Closes her umbrella*.)

PETER. Is that how you felt? Left behind? (*Closes his umbrella*.)

DAHLIA. That's how I feel now. But as the one leaving.

PETER. And you won't give that up, hence the self-hatred.

DAHLIA. If I'm fortunate, it will dissipate . . . just as it has for you. It's a complicated problem, isn't it?

PETER. Yeah, it's really complicated, Dahlia. Journalists also die and are imprisoned and tortured.

DAHLIA. Not us.

PETER. Would death have made me a better person in your eyes?

DAHLIA. It would have erased all the questions and all the flaws.

PETER. It will pass.

DAHLIA. What will?

PETER. Your guilt.

DAHLIA. Has yours? Completely?

PETER. No.

DAHLIA. Guilt's complicated. Laila's executor wanted to save her, but he killed her in the end. In Sarajevo, I saw people die and I saw people kill. If you had died I would have carried any recollection of you in merely the very best of memories, even if those memories were imagined. We feel guilty for killing . . . for death . . . for abandonment . . . but make ourselves believe it's the only way to save . . . the other . . . the other we don't know or understand.

PETER. I knew you. I understood you.

DAHLIA. It's all right, Peter. I know what we do now. I understand it. I don't begrudge you for it. But I know it has to come to an end. Those faces can't stay clipped to our conscience forever.

PETER. You have.

DAHLIA. Why?

PETER. You questioned me . . . even in Sarajevo, you called me on everything, my motivation, my intentions. No one else did. My wife never has. What could be . . . dishonorable in what we do? Isn't it all for the good of the cause? I'm not sorry for what I've done or written, or for the acclaim it brought me. But I took my own advice, and stopped, because I've chosen to stop listening. I don't want to hear it anymore. I teach others who want to become you what questions they should ask and how to ask them. But I leave all . . . this out of the lecture. You can't teach guilt or loss or fear, or even regret. And speaking of regret, I regret coming here today, because you've reminded me of all I left behind. (*Crosses to stage left, on his way out.*)

Dahlia catches up with him and hits him.

DAHLIA. You told me to write. You told me to stay and tell stories, which I've finally done. The only difference is, there are more of us now, with more to tell. We talk about guilt and regret? You're the same person I met years ago, wracked with guilt for even coming today, for even having this conversation with me. But it's a false guilt, because it will disappear the moment you turn away from me. Just like my guilt is also false, because I benefit from others' stories, their loss. But I still write and accept invitations to bookstores in New York and other exciting cities, so I can read my words and enjoy listening to myself and sell what I've written and sign my name and speak to you. Maybe we're the same person, and that's what draws us to each other. Maybe we're nothing more than our reflection of each other. Maybe that's all we've ever been. (*Crosses right.*)

PETER (*calls after her*). And perhaps you'll find someone to have this conversation with in another twelve years, and your role will be reversed because you'll want this to end.

DAHLIA (*shouts back*). As you have.

Peter approaches Dahlia with a copy of her book.

PETER (*shouts*). Could you sign it?

DAHLIA (*shouts*). Of course. (*Signs Peter's book and hands it back to him.*)

PETER. *Hvala*. What are you thanking me for?

DAHLIA. Telling me to stay and write my own story.

The End

PARADISE

CHARACTERS

MEENA	Female
RAJ	Male

SETTINGS

Meena's grave

Bedroom in Meena and Raj's home country

Cramped apartment in Katrina-ravaged New Orleans

Dark room in Meena's home country

NOTES ON THE PLAY

Paradise premiered at the Looking Glass Theatre, New York, on November 29, 2007, with the following cast and crew:

Meena	Beth Jastroch
Raj	Joe Cappelli
Assistant Directors	Margot Fitzsimmons
	Laura Neuhaus
Lighting Director	Ryan Metzler
Producer	Aliza Shane
Director	Jacquelyn Honeybourne

The present. Meena speaks to the audience from underground, where she has been buried alive, after being stoned. Pebbles, rocks, and dirt surround her; she uses the dirt and sand as her security blanket, running her fingers through the grain and smoothing it over her naked arms and legs.

MEENA. He told me my voice was like a razor, my vision was unclear, and that I was a child who knew nothing about anything. I was an adolescent in a woman's body, and that wasn't right, so he would teach me. I would be his challenge. He told me he loved me, and a lot of other things. He said that I was . . . different . . . looked different, talked different, sounded different, thought different, ate different. "Odd? Strange?" "No, just . . . better." "Better than what?" "Than what I've known." (*Beat.*) He told me that loving him wouldn't have been so dangerous, and that our . . . differences, his religion and mine, were merely words—futile. Absolutely nothing! Nothing of substance. And that no one really cared anymore. What a joke! He told me that I would be a fool, a lonely fool to be so concerned. And who was the fool again? He had no idea. But he discovered later on that . . . we . . . couldn't . . . be. Not there. So maybe, here? He would save me, you see, by taking me away and bringing me to another place, city, district, strangeness, mess, that was never supposed to be this . . . mess. And that he knew someone who knew someone who knew someone else here, and all would be fine. Identity? Papers? Status? There are always ways around those very trivial concerns. And identity is the size of a grain of sand? Even now. Despite everything we think, there's always a way. Even now. (*Sand and pebbles pour through her fingers.*) And had we stayed back home, a thousand small stones would have been thrown at me until I had fallen dead into the ground, or perhaps, buried alive. What would that have been like, I wondered? I laughed and said, "At least it would have been a dry ground!" Raj didn't think it was funny. But I did. (*Beat.*) He feared being found there and sent back here. He feared being nothing, but for myself, I welcomed it, being nothing. Feeling nothing. Absent. And was he something here? Were we? We're drowning. We're being buried alive. We've escaped one honorable killing for this one. We're being sealed within this room, within this grave, on this pyre. But there is no honor. There was no honor, not on a village dirt road and not on the Mississippi. Nowhere. To be buried in an unmarked grave in the river, bereft of ash, fire, shroud, dirt, just tears and the water. It's appealing to have never been known. To be in a place where you never existed, to be buried alive, to be stoned, to drown, all in a place where no one outside your tomb breathed your name or touched your skin, or heard your voice; perhaps heard, but not listened. Where you were nothing. And had we stayed? Had I been . . . underground . . . beneath a pile of dirt on a village road, I would have asked him, "Can you hear me? I can hear you. Listen. I would have felt you. I would have spoken had you brushed past me. Had I still . . . been. But here I am, under the pebbles, under the sand, without light, without breath, with a name, with a place, without honor, with shame. Shame for having loved you, more than I or you or anyone could understand. With air and time running out, here I stand. A citizen, with shame, self-imposed shame, they say. On my knees, face to the ground, mouth in the dirt, skin torn by pebbles and shards of glass, tossed into my grave, dug by my hands, my nails, myself. All for love? Honor? Shame? Stripped of citizenship and home, and buried without a name." (*Beat.*) Look at what you've saved me from—all that! Thank you.

PART 2. Home

The past. A bedroom in Meena and Raj's home country. Meena stands at the foot of the bed, while Raj is in bed.

RAJ. Come back.

MEENA. No.

RAJ. Why?

MEENA. Because I'm afraid.

RAJ. Of me?

MEENA. Of where I am.

RAJ. Well, you were in my bed, and now you're not. Now you're standing away from me, looking down on me.

MEENA. It's this place.

RAJ. This place. This secretive, hidden, evil, sad place.

MEENA. I never said that.

RAJ. And I never forced you.

MEENA. You did. (*Beat.*) You did and you didn't.

RAJ. Dangerous words coming from your mouth. You should watch what you say and who's around to hear them.

MEENA. That's not what I meant. I would never . . .

RAJ. What? Hurt me? Have me hurt?

MEENA. You know I wouldn't.

RAJ. Sad. Always so damn sad.

MEENA. And how should I be?

RAJ. A little . . . happy?

MEENA. Like in the movies?

RAJ. That'd be nice.

MEENA. Shall I do a little dance now? A little post-intercourse Bolly act? Why don't we get some musicians from off the street to join us?

RAJ. Why not?

MEENA. I almost forgot everything else, just for a moment.

RAJ. You can. It's not supposed to be like this.

MEENA. Well with me it is, and you chose me. You saw me first! You saw me before I saw you. You spoke to me first! You saw me, and you knew me. You knew what I was! So deal with it!

RAJ. They've really fucked you up, haven't they? Your family, your people, your . . . whoever . . . whatever! But maybe it's you! Maybe it's your head. Hell, maybe they're not even so bad. Maybe they'd extend an arm upon meeting me, and ask me to tea. Maybe it's all you. Maybe you like this.

MEENA. You know nothing.

RAJ. I'm glad. I'm glad I don't have to live in your skin, in your head, and know your fear, whether it's real or imaginary. I wouldn't want to know.

MEENA. But you will.

RAJ. Real or imaginary?

MEENA. Both.

RAJ. Why be here with me?

MEENA. Because I wanted to.

RAJ. Something to get over and done with, right?

MEENA. I wanted you.

RAJ. The evil bastard who has no sympathy, who basically calls you paranoid and your family crazy.

MEENA. That's right.

RAJ (*grabs Meena and pulls her onto the bed*). How do I love someone who fears me?

MEENA. You don't love me. You can't.

RAJ. Why can't I?

MEENA. I'm unlovable.

RAJ. That's easier to be, isn't it? All your problems are solved. All your worries erased. Safe.

MEENA. That's why I said it.

RAJ. You're not unlovable.

MEENA. I wish I could be happy.

RAJ. You could be. You could forget, like before. Just for a moment. Just for now.

MEENA. I was stupid, and it has nothing to do with you.

RAJ. Of course, it's all me. But who's going to know anything?

MEENA. People always know, in the end. They sense it. No words even have to be said aloud. They know. You're not afraid?

RAJ. Of what?

MEENA. Of being hurt.

RAJ. By them or by you?

MEENA. I wouldn't hurt you.

RAJ. Not intentionally.

MEENA. You should worry about them.

RAJ. Why? Are you going to turn me in?

MEENA. Are you crazy?

RAJ. Obviously.

MEENA (*warms to Raj*). Yes, very obviously.

RAJ. Anyway. I like danger.

MEENA. The big screen kind or the real-life kind?

RAJ. None of it. I like you.

MEENA. Oh. The real-life kind, because liking me would be very dangerous.

RAJ. It shouldn't matter.

MEENA. But it does.

RAJ. Not to me.

MEENA. But to a lot of other people.

RAJ. The simple? Humble? Poor? Uneducated? The cave dwellers?

MEENA. You'd be surprised.

RAJ. What if we're all cave dwellers? Everyone in the world? And we, the ones who think we're not, try to spend our lives pretending we know something else? Something more? Something better? When, in fact, we know nothing.

MEENA. We don't know anything, except what we want, or what we think we want.

RAJ. What do you think you want? A happy arrangement? A big wedding?

MEENA. To go to a place where no one knows I exist.

RAJ. What?

MEENA. You asked.

RAJ. I expected to hear a thousand pieces of gold, white elephants . . .

MEENA. No. I want to go and live in a place where no one knows I was ever born, ever existed.

RAJ. Impossible.

MEENA. Not if I'm invisible. I'd walk the strange streets and no one would see me, feel me.

RAJ. Then you'd be nothing.

MEENA. That's right! Untouchable. Left alone. No evidence. No bloody sheets to wash, lies to tell, stones to duck from. Dust. No, more than dust, or actually less than dust. Nothing.

RAJ. I don't believe you.

MEENA. Then don't. It's my head. My thoughts. But you should understand.

RAJ. Why?

MEENA. Because you're invisible here. Nothing.

RAJ. That's not the same.

MEENA. You can't cross over to be something else, someone else, no matter, how much you know, or think you know. And that's why you want to leave.

RAJ. Dust, nothingness can't be loved, can't be touched.

MEENA. Another benefit. Another sense of ease, without guilt.

RAJ. You feel guilt for being with me?

MEENA. Another wish. I wish I could be happy. I wish I weren't guilty. I wish I were nothing. But it's all in my head, right?

RAJ. I suppose it comes from somewhere.

MEENA. It's real. All of it.

RAJ. And now you can pass it on to me. Am I your excuse?

MEENA. What?

RAJ. Am I your excuse to run away? Just as you could be my excuse to finally leave.

MEENA. Who's running? I never said anything about . . . leaving.

RAJ. But that's what this is, your wishes, your fears. I'm the voice you need to hear to pass through the gate. "Go on. Don't look back. Forget them." Just as you're my voice reminding me that I'm nothing in this place. And that I'll remain, as . . . dust, if I stay here, and that nothing in my life will change, will get better, no matter how much I know, or think I know, unless, I go.

MEENA. It never crossed my mind.

RAJ. You're a liar.

MEENA. I'm not. Well, I have become one.

RAJ. Because of me? How long can you keep this going?

MEENA. Not much longer.

RAJ. Lying can be exhausting.

MEENA. I wouldn't know. I never thought of any of this as lying. I've always pretended to be someone else, something else.

RAJ. Who were you?

MEENA. Anyone but me. Any other skin, or name, or religion, or home, or family, or culture . . . any but my own.

RAJ. You hated yourself?

MEENA. I don't know if it was or is hatred.

RAJ. Are you still pretending?

MEENA. Not to you.

RAJ. So this is real?

MEENA. I've been so distant from what's real. I think it is. I hope it is.

RAJ. So say it.

MEENA. What?

RAJ. Go on.

MEENA. Where?

RAJ. Away from here.

MEENA. A mythical, magical place, where we could be lost.

RAJ. Say it.

MEENA. And I'm the mad one?

RAJ. Let's go.

MEENA. Let go?

RAJ. No. Let us go.

    They kiss and fall into each other.

PART 3. Paradise

The past. A cramped apartment in New Orleans, ravaged by Hurricane Katrina.

MEENA (*lighting candles on a dark stage, as the only light appears on her*). It's strange who our sages are, in what forms they appear, what voices they use. They're never what we imagine wisdom and superior knowledge to be. We think of that old man in the village square who sits for endless hours with his cane, chewing tobacco, his face lined like the rings of a tree stump that's stood . . . forever. Just like the stump, that old fake sage has probably sat in that same sorry chair forever, in that same cow dung-caked spot. He advises us, admonishes us, warns us. But, in the end, he knows nothing. Just like those fools in the tall offices and in the newspapers and on the television screens who bombard us with . . . nonsense. It's nonsense because they know nothing too. And perhaps we're the greater fools because we think they, the old man and our soulless puppets, actually know something. Something that should be revealed to us and direct us! I was mistaken. I should have listened to my sages, the real ones. They were trying to warn me that "this" was coming . . . this hell that would use water instead of fire to burn us and swallow us up. And that's what's funny about this . . . freakish existence . . . because that's where they magically appeared to me. My sages. On Governor Nicholls Wharf along the Mississippi River that morning before these past bizarre mornings in hell. New Orleans isn't a morning city because morning is too damn honest. Morning doesn't give us the time to make up the stories we're going to tell about ourselves later that day. It presents us in our most . . . brutally raw and ugly forms. I didn't want to go to work that morning. I too was dressed by seven in my brutally raw and ugly form in my hotel-maid uniform. I felt ugly inside and out. I don't know why. I just felt, and walked, in that heat, that very familiar, brutal heat. And then, they appeared, my sages. One of them a fourteen-foot alligator frighteningly close to the edge of the wharf. I thought he was chasing me. I'd never seen anything like him. He was sharp and angry, but focused, focused on this . . . mission, this mission he had to accomplish, that no one could understand because to him we didn't count, not I nor any other spectator walking along the river that morning. But he knew what he had to do. I looked at him, wondering why he was there. And then I saw her. My second sage. She was his mission. She was his focus. She was what led him to the rocky edge of the river. She was a black cat. The most beautiful creature I had ever seen, with a coat of the most beautiful and blackest fur. Her body, emaciated body but her eyes piercing, looking at you, the spectator, pleading to be saved from his sharpness and his anger and his deadly intent. He went below the water when he saw that she'd spotted him, that she knew he was there. He let her think she was safe for a moment, but then she'd stumble on the rocks. And the second she stumbled

and showed her vulnerability . . . No, not weakness, but her
. . . trust . . . he'd appear, causing her to scramble backwards,
higher up on the rocks, away from him. She wasn't vulnerable or weak. She was good. She was trusting. She believed
that perhaps he really wouldn't hurt her. But it was all a game
for him. Who was she? Where did she come from? Who
owned her? Did anyone? And why did he want her so much?
A few other spectators—some public workers—came to
watch, and laughed. It was a show for them, a free spectacle.
They were more excited by the fourteen-foot alligator, but I
was fixed on her. We followed them, this odd pair. I should
have done something. I should have scooped her up and run.
But I was afraid of him, of how fast he would be, of what he
would do to me if I got too close. The others just smiled and
laughed at the two of them. I didn't want to see what he
would do to her. I was the coward, so I ran away. I'm sure he
caught her, frightened her, fulfilled his mission, killed her. She
lost before she was even born. She had no chance.

PART 4. Hell

*The past. Lights up on the stage. Meena is on a mattress on the floor,
next to Raj. It is a one-room apartment in New Orleans with a single
window. A stool is by the window. The apartment is already flooded. The
walls, covered with newspaper and magazine photographs of Bollywood
actors, are wet. There are empty beer cans and a compact, empty refrigerator. There is no electricity, nor running water. Obviously unable to
wash, Meena and Raj are in filthy undergarments. Raj is in boxer
shorts, while Meena wears a bra and panties. Raj is asleep. Meena
shakes Raj's shoulder.*

RAJ. What?

MEENA. We have to leave. (*Raj turns away from Meena and tries to
sleep.*) We have to leave, now!

RAJ. No, we don't!

MEENA. Raj . . .

RAJ. Don't call my name this early.

MEENA. You're hiding.

RAJ. Your voice is like a razor.

MEENA. And you've lost your will to see what's in front of you.

RAJ (*sits up*). I see nothing.

MEENA. Then you're blind or crazy.

RAJ. Can't I be both? (*Rises and walks towards the refrigerator. Meena follows.*) There's nothing to eat.

MEENA. There's been nothing to eat.

RAJ. Since when?

MEENA. Since two days ago. (*Grabbing Raj's arm*) Please. Let's go.

RAJ. To where, Meena?

MEENA. Anywhere.

> *Raj returns to bed. Meena follows.*

RAJ (*soothes Meena by stroking her hair*). Fall back. Close your eyes. Don't look outside. Don't look at the ground or the walls or what's above us. Don't look at anything. Don't listen to anything, and it will be over soon.

MEENA (*walks to the window*). So you finally admit there's something happening.

RAJ. I'm just trying to make you happy.

MEENA. Happy? Is that what I'm supposed to feel? Let's just . . . go. I see rafts . . . people trying to get out.

RAJ. They're not us.

MEENA. Maybe they are.

RAJ. Then they're fools.

MEENA. They just want to live.

RAJ. They want to be caught.

MEENA. They won't be.

IMAGE 4.1 **Raj refuses to escape their drowning city.**
Beth Jastroch as Meena and Joe Cappelli as Raj.
Paradise, Looking Glass Theatre, New York, November 29, 2007.
Photograph by Natalie Golonka.

RAJ. Oh, they will be. Anytime, even drowning time, is a good trapping time, especially now.

MEENA. But we could be anyone. We wouldn't have to be ourselves, just anyone else.

RAJ (*rises, takes a beer can from the floor, brings it to his lips, notices it's empty and is frustrated*). Just anyone? "What's your name? Where do you live? You don't sound like you're from here. What's your social security number? Driver's license? Oh, so when did you come to this country? Don't remember? Well, how did you get here? Can't remember that either? Why are you here? Really here? Let me check you out, ah, so you're really not supposed to be here, are you?!" (*Throws the empty beer can.*)

MEENA. You think people care now?

RAJ. Now? Yes. This is the only time they'd care about people like us. The only time they'd look at people like us. And a broken levee and a river rising wouldn't make any difference!

MEENA. Okay. So we leave, and crawl out, and board a raft, and they ask, and we answer, that we have no name here, no one waiting for us, no papers, no identity, no plan, no present, no future. We answer every interrogation because there's nothing else to say.

RAJ. Nothing to say? Then you're just like the other fools!

MEENA. You're cruel.

RAJ. I'm just honest.

MEENA. What were you ever doing with me?

Beat.

RAJ (*holding Meena by the shoulders, takes her back to the mattress*). I . . . I didn't mean what I said.

MEENA. Yes, you did.

RAJ (*rising*). You're not in my head! You can't know what I think!

MEENA. You didn't answer me! Why me in the first place? Was it because of how I looked or how I didn't look? Or because of the danger? Does it fascinate you? Did I?

RAJ. You were never a game!

MEENA. That doesn't matter! It was still a risk and I'm asking you if that's what made you want me! What made you approach me? Made you look at me? See me? Just like staying in this room and waiting to drown, or starve, or kill, or be killed! Is that what turns you on?

RAJ. I saved you.

MEENA. Not at this moment.

RAJ. You would have been dead if you had stayed. Your family was going to kill you.

MEENA. Because of you.

RAJ. I loved you.

MEENA. And now? (*Raj breaks away from Meena, unable to answer.*) I know. Me too. It's all so obscure now. I know what I want to feel, but I'm afraid it's been lost in this room these past two days. I can't remember what I used to fear, before, this.

RAJ. You still fear.

MEENA. Now I'm being selfish. It's a selfish fear.

RAJ. And back home you were being honorable? So that's why you had to leave? Because staying would have been, dishonorable?

MEENA. There was no honor. There is no honor, especially not at this moment. How could there be?

RAJ. You blame me for everything.

MEENA. I did what I wanted.

RAJ. You could still do what you want.

MEENA. What are you saying?

RAJ. You want to go, Meena? Then go. I'll help you. We'll break that window, and I'll hold onto you and throw you out into your . . . anywhere . . . where you could be . . . "just anyone" . . . anyone other than who you really are. (*Beat. He looks out of the window.*) Any order just . . . seeps away. If there was ever any order. This chaos prevents you from doing anything . . . that was . . . usual, normal. You can't count time anymore, because it doesn't mean anything. There's no place you have to get to . . . no job . . . no . . . meal waiting for you at home . . . maybe there's no one waiting for you at home. You say I've lost the will to see? I can't see. I can't see anything, except for the people we once knew who are floating around us, but we can't respond, because we can't feel. (*Turning to Meena*) I don't know what else brought me to you. I'm sorry. I can't remember.

MEENA. That's all right. (*Beat.*) Raj, there's nothing left to drink.

RAJ (*confused*). What?

MEENA. No water. Not the good kind. No more beer. Nothing else.

RAJ (*distant*). That's too bad.

MEENA. You'd rather . . . drown . . . die than be questioned? After everything it took to come here?

RAJ. Yeah.

MEENA. You really believe that?

RAJ. I've believed worse.

MEENA. There was never really a chance.

RAJ. For what?

MEENA. To be like everyone else.

RAJ. Oh, everyone else here? Everyone else who was transmitted to us with their false names and places and houses in magical and mythical villages that don't drown? The ones whom we believed were real?

MEENA. It was a dream . . . a stupid one.

RAJ. Are you sorry?

MEENA. For what?

RAJ. Coming here?

MEENA. No. But I'll be sorry for dying here. I've become like you . . . nothing's clear anymore.

RAJ. We have to stay.

MEENA. What are you so afraid of? Your loss of pride that this false dream didn't work out?

RAJ. Confinement. Return.

MEENA. We're not criminals.

RAJ. We're illegal, not legal. Wrong, not right.

MEENA. That's never frightened you these past six months.

RAJ. Maybe it did, but I didn't know, not until now. I won't be caught. I won't be held. I won't go back. I have nothing to go back to.

MEENA. And you have something here?

RAJ. No, I don't.

MEENA. Why stay? Do you have . . . hope?

RAJ. No. I just want to be still.

MEENA. You're such a liar! You don't want to waste the money you spent in getting us here! That's all this is! You can't admit loss, defeat! What confinement? Return? That's the fear?

RAJ. I was nothing!

MEENA. And what are you here? (*Raj breaks down and falls onto the mattress. She follows.*) The fear is us, here, at this time, seeing and hearing what's outside that window. Seeing what's inside this room. Feeling . . . trapped. And not knowing what to do.

RAJ. Do you want to leave?

MEENA. Do you?

RAJ (*slowly and deliberately*). No.

Meena collapses in grief.

MEENA. How could you have done everything you've done and come this far to end, to end it now, like this?

RAJ. You can go.

MEENA. I want you to answer me!

RAJ. I can't.

MEENA (*rising, emotionally*). Maybe this isn't happening and there really isn't any flooding, any drowning. Maybe we're imagining this and this isn't real.

RAJ. But it is.

MEENA. You want to kill yourself, and maybe, me, also. But you're too much of a coward to do it directly, so you do it like this. You wait for death to come for us!

RAJ. Why would I do that?

MEENA. Confinement, return, fear, false identities, no identities, white elephants, none of it . . . all of it? Only you know.

RAJ. We've lost.

MEENA. I loved you too.

RAJ. I know you did.

MEENA (*approaches Raj*). I don't regret following you here.

RAJ. That admission makes all of this a speck better.

MEENA. This is real. I believe that. That's all I can believe now, that this is really happening.

RAJ. Then I believe it also.

MEENA. And if we don't leave now, we'll die. Can you believe that?

RAJ. Wouldn't this be an appropriate way to end, looking back on how we began and where that's brought us?

MEENA (*breaking*). I don't want to be finished.

RAJ. You or us?

MEENA. Both. You're so frightened of leaving?

RAJ. And you're so frightened of staying?

MEENA. I lied. (*Meena takes a beer can from under the mattress.*) But that's all there is.

RAJ. You keep it.

MEENA. We could share.

RAJ. I don't want it.

MEENA (*opens the bottle and begins to drink. Both sit on the mattress and are severely feeling the effects of heat, and lack of food and water*). You were the smartest person I had ever met.

RAJ. Were?

MEENA. Up until now.

RAJ. Thanks.

MEENA. I remember our first night here, when I looked up into the sky and counted the stars and thought, "I can't believe I'm here and I'm under this sky and these stars," and how it really didn't look so different from home. And maybe it wouldn't be so different from home, and sometimes it wasn't—this heat —sometimes oppressive—was familiar—in some ways.

RAJ. Not familiar enough.

MEENA. There aren't any more stars to count.

RAJ. There are. You've just forgotten how to count them.

MEENA. Or I don't want to, anymore.

RAJ. More stupid dreams?

MEENA (*stumbles to the window*). It's getting worse.

RAJ. Monsoons? Floods? Yeah, maybe this is familiar.

MEENA. Not here. Not like this. Come look. (*Raj stumbles to join Meena at the window.*) You're not scared?

RAJ (*coldly*). I'm not anything.. . . . Everyone should know his own place, right? You look at me and think I don't know who I am or where I belong, or where I feel . . . safe . . . home. And I look at you and think I wish I could be like her. And even though you want something so . . . distant . . . so unattainable . . . you believe you can have it; that it's yours, just as much as it is anyone else's, and that no one would say you can't have it. You think I have a death wish, that I want to die and take you along with me. But I don't. Not really. I don't want to starve or drown. Yet I don't want to be confined or sent back to where I was nothing. Nothing? Does that make me "something" here? Probably not. When I walked these streets as me, me before the flood, the people in this place would walk right past me. Our bodies may have touched in passing but the people here would never realize it, wouldn't see it, wouldn't feel it, because they wouldn't see . . . or feel me. Maybe you don't either. Maybe you never have, and that's why you can turn away from me and leave. So what will be left? What will my legacy be? Cigarette butts and ashes in a sink with no water? A garbage bag filled with all worldly possessions? A beer-stained floating mattress in the river? A whisper, saying, "Go on." You think I'm cruel. You think I have no heart, no feeling. But I look at you and wonder, "How will she remember me?" What will our legacy be? This room? These ashes? This heat? This bed? This . . . nothingness? You'll go on and on. Perhaps in many years to come, I'll diminish in your memory, so much so that . . . you may even have trouble remembering my voice, my face, even my name, whichever name you wish to recall. And if I were to live and we were to pass each other on the street in this city, when all is almost forgotten, until the next disaster, maybe you too would brush past me, as the others so easily can, and feel . . . nothing. Maybe you'll become them. Maybe. Or perhaps not. I hope not. I don't know. Terrible events have always happened. People have always been denied entry. People have always drowned . . . have always . . . been left . . . diminished . . . doubted . . . if they were even real, if they even existed. Without a name, a name someone can call out in the street without fear of being found, without an identity, it's easy to question your existence. Am I really here? There's no evidence saying that I am. No one knows me. No one feels me. Maybe I'll be remembered as a bad dream . . . something that can't really hurt you, because a dream is what's . . . imagined . . . untouchable . . . unreal.

MEENA (*draws Raj close to her; slowly, deliberately, powerfully*). We have to leave . . . Now.

RAJ. At least you've woken up. You've come out of your deep sleep of fear. Fear of being stoned. Fear of being discovered. Fear of being touched, of being held, being loved. Fear of staying. Fear of returning. All gone.

MEENA. It's not gone, because I don't want to die.

RAJ. And it's taken you this . . . bizarre moment to realize that.

MEENA. I've never wanted to die.

RAJ. "Dust." No, "Less than dust. Nothing." (*Blows.*) Poof. Your words. Your wishes.

MEENA. I only wanted a different life from the one I had.

RAJ. Well, you got it.

MEENA. We say things we don't mean.

RAJ. We do mean them. Maybe we mean them as much as the size of a speck, dust. That's the only part we mean; the rest of it just words, but the truth's still there, hidden, hiding.

MEENA. I wanted to be free.

RAJ. You've got that too! This is what freedom is, don't you know? What it looks like, tastes like, without all the confines of name and place and religion and money and no money and opportunity and no opportunity and being something and being nothing! This is it! This is what we've wanted! Embrace it!

MEENA. This isn't what it was supposed to be. It's all wrong.

RAJ. It was never right, Meena, from the beginning. I loved you. I may still, but I can't see anymore. I can't think clearly, except know I did love you and also used you, as you used me. We did this to each other.

MEENA. Come with me! We could stay . . . invisible, imaginary, unreal. Never found, never known, just as we've been. It could be nice, even better, because we've seen what could be worse. This is worse! Now is worse! This must be . . . hell. I'll be better. I'll be more, more lovable, less fearful. I promise you. I'll be like everyone else, like those girls in the movies you love. I'll never worry. I'll never think of the past, or look over my shoulder, or cry at night. I'll always smile. I'll never be serious, never fret, never be sad. Never again. There'd be nothing to cry about because we'd be nothing . . . to all of them, here, there. But to us . . . we'd be alive.

RAJ. Nothing to them? Just as I was back home? And am now again? And again? And again? And again? No. No more.

MEENA. We're in hell.

RAJ. But it's familiar. Home.

MEENA. Yours. But not mine.

RAJ. It's your punishment, for loving me.

MEENA. My life is my punishment for loving you. Being in my head, my skin, that's my punishment, the real one, without the stones and dirt, and Mississippi. But why make it worse than it is, with drowning? It's already here; it's already been handed down, my sentence, so why would I want to sharpen the objects of execution? Why would you?

RAJ. Meena, I'll be your voice, just as before. Listen. Your whisper, saying, "Go on."

MEENA. No.

RAJ. You listened in the past. You risked everything to be touched, to be held, to be loved. You risked hell, being buried alive. Buried alive! You've already won! Why risk being buried alive here, when you defeated it there? That would be tragic. More tragic than never having left home. Even more tragic than letting me go, because I want to be let go.

MEENA. You didn't come all this way and risk everything to be let go!

IMAGE 4.2 **Meena looks beyond New Orleans for hope.**
Beth Jastroch as Meena and Joe Cappelli as Raj.
Paradise, Looking Glass Theatre, New York, November 29, 2007.
Photograph by Natalie Golonka.

RAJ. I risked nothing.

MEENA. Confinement. Dishonor. Death.

RAJ. I failed.

MEENA. And I'll fail if I go, if I leave you.

MEENA'S INTERROGATION

Meena sits on the stool. Raj stands before her and takes on the role of Interrogator as Meena takes on that of Prisoner.

RAJ. Go on.

MEENA. Am I underground? Am I being buried alive? Are they throwing rocks and dirt over me?

RAJ. Did you let him touch you?

MEENA. Yes.

RAJ. Did you give your body to him?

MEENA. Yes.

RAJ. Did anyone else know or aid in your relationship?

MEENA. He knew people.

RAJ. Friends of his?

MEENA. Yes.

RAJ. They lied for him, as you deceived your family? Shamed them?

MEENA. That wasn't my intention.

RAJ. What did you say?

MEENA. Yes, they lied for us.

RAJ. Why did you do it?

MEENA. I don't know.

RAJ. Did he force you?

MEENA. No.

RAJ. Never?

MEENA. Never.

RAJ. Where did you first meet?

MEENA. The cinema . . . movies.

RAJ. What were you watching?

MEENA. A . . . Bollywood movie. A silly, stupid, movie. It meant nothing.

RAJ. A love story?

MEENA. Of course.

RAJ. You both like the movies?

MEENA. Very much so.

RAJ. Where was he sitting?

MEENA. Across from me.

RAJ. Who spoke first?

MEENA. He did.

RAJ. Before? During? After the film?

MEENA. After.

RAJ. You told him your name?

MEENA. Yes.

RAJ. Your real name?

MEENA. Yes.

RAJ. And he told you his?

MEENA. Yes.

RAJ. And yet, you continued to let him speak to you?

MEENA. Yes.

RAJ. You wanted him to?

MEENA (*whispering*). I did.

RAJ. Louder!

MEENA. Yes! I wanted him to speak to me. I wanted to speak to him.

RAJ. And that was it?

MEENA. Yes, that was it.

RAJ. You didn't think it was wrong?

MEENA. I did, but . . .

RAJ. But what?

MEENA. I didn't care.

RAJ. You knew what the consequences of your actions would be?

MEENA. I knew. I know.

RAJ. And yet, you continued. For how long until you both ran away?

MEENA. One year.

RAJ. One year. You both lied for one year.

MEENA. Yes we did.

RAJ. Why did you do it?

MEENA. Because I wanted to be loved, by him, and . . . I wanted to love him. That was all.

RAJ. That was all?

MEENA. Yes.

RAJ. Did you hate your family so much to dishonor them and yourself?

MEENA. I hated myself, not them.

RAJ. So that's why you let him touch you, out of self-hatred?

MEENA. Yes, but not to continue my hatred—to end it. I wanted it to end, and I thought the only way for that to happen was to be loved and touched and to let someone in, someone who wouldn't hurt me.

RAJ. But he has hurt you. Look where you are, now. Perhaps you wanted to end your life but didn't have the courage to do it, so you . . . continued to be loved and touched, and let the responsibility, go into the hands of another? Just perhaps.

MEENA. I don't want to die. And I don't want to be invisible, not anymore.

RAJ. But that's exactly what's going to happen.

MEENA. Would you allow that to happen to me?

RAJ. It's not my decision.

MEENA. What will happen to him?

RAJ. The same as what will happen to you.

MEENA. He was foolish.

RAJ. He was.

MEENA. He didn't truly understand, everything. He thought he did, but he didn't.

RAJ. Did it have a happy ending?

MEENA. What?

RAJ. Your movie at the cinema that night.

MEENA. I don't remember.

RAJ. Of course you do.

MEENA (*tearfully*). Yes. Yes it did.

RAJ. That's good, then.

MEENA. It was, and it can be.

HURRICANE KATRINA

Meena and Raj cease to be Interrogator and Prisoner. Meena leaves the stool and Raj crumbles to the floor.

MEENA. Are we underground? Are we being buried alive? Are they throwing rocks and dirt over us? Have we drowned in these strange waters with their strange sounds and talk? Are we finished?

RAJ. Not yet. But we will be if you stay and they see me with you.

MEENA. Don't be afraid. They've already seen us. They know.

RAJ. This is hell, and it's not where you belong. So you have to go—now.

MEENA. Let's go, then.

RAJ. No, Meena. Let go.

MEENA. Now it's your turn. Take my hand, and come with me, and don't be afraid, of anything. Let me love you. Do you believe me? Do you believe us? There are worse enemies than law and stones and status. Take my hand and let's go.

RAJ. But I don't know what I'm doing anymore.

MEENA. You don't have to, for now. Just come with me. It hasn't ended.

Raj embraces Meena.

THE CAGE

Raj reverts to the role of Interrogator and Meena to that of Prisoner.

RAJ. And what happened next?

MEENA. The real ending? Without the white elephants and pieces of gold? He looked into my eyes and said, "I'm sorry. I'm really sorry." He had lost. He was lost, and he couldn't find his way back, so he surrendered and removed his hand from mine and climbed back into the cage: our bed, a bed of emptiness, nothingness, familiarity, home.

RAJ. Hell.

MEENA. Just as I now sit in your cage.

RAJ. He hurt you.

MEENA. No, not really. I know that was all he could do. I thought we were free, from the past, but here, there, in a crowd of unfamiliar sounds and voices, he became, confused, embittered, hopeless. They followed us. You followed us.

RAJ. Why didn't you kill yourself? Not in America, but here, before America, when you started with him?

MEENA. Why?

RAJ. Because that would have been the right thing to do.

MEENA. So I could lessen your guilt in having to kill me?

RAJ. I carry no guilt.

MEENA. You will.

Beat.

RAJ. Where did you go, after his . . . apology?

MEENA. I wanted to climb inside with him, and wrap my body around his, hold him, close everything out, see nothing, hear nothing, fear nothing.

RAJ. Feel nothing?

MEENA. I thought I did, but then I didn't. I didn't want to lose that. But I wanted to lose everything else, just for a moment, and then I stopped myself. I couldn't stay in there with him.

RAJ. Sure you could have. Then you wouldn't have found yourself back here, with me.

MEENA. I would have been finished.

RAJ. But you will be.

MEENA. But not there.

RAJ. And you didn't have the courage he did.

MEENA. Is that what he had?

RAJ. He showed honor.

MEENA. He did? To what? To whom? To you? Was it for you I should have stayed in that bed with him?

RAJ. You thought flight would have saved you. Your flight to and from that hell.

MEENA. It did.

RAJ. For a moment. For a second. You thought those you were running to would be your protectors, better than we, than I. You thought they would be your salvation. But they weren't, because after everything, they sent you right back here, to your blood, to your enemy.

MEENA. You're not my enemy. You're him, the only one I've ever loved. You're myself. We've all found ourselves in the same place now.

RAJ. Don't try to place yourself in my favor, because I won't save you.

MEENA. I'm not asking you to. I stopped trying to put myself in anyone's favor, grace, a long time ago. I can't remember when the pretense ended.

RAJ. Now you're back to being yourself.

MEENA. You see why I don't care anymore?

RAJ. I'm curious what you did between the time you climbed out of your cage in paradise and into this cage in hell with me?

MEENA. That too was hell. It became hell.

RAJ (*whispering*). What did you do?

MEENA. I wandered.

RAJ. Did he cry before you left?

MEENA. Oh no. He was very still and just stared at the ceiling, without motion, without sound. I couldn't even hear him breathe. Maybe he didn't. Maybe he was already gone.

RAJ. Maybe he cried for you when you left?

MEENA. Why would you want him to cry?

RAJ. Not for me, but for you. To show you he really loved you.

MEENA. He did. One time, he did.

RAJ. I believe you.

MEENA. I climbed through the window and wandered, past the river, engulfed in the river, in heat, in emptiness, screams, silence, violence, quiet. All of it. But I didn't stop. I didn't want to be still, not out of fear of what would happen, but because of what had just happened. I didn't want to think about him, wonder, remember, regret. All I can say, is it was gone, any trust I had in any person or system or country. Gone. He did that to me. Or rather, I let him take that away from me. It was completely broken off, belief in any one person or thing whether it be God, home, family, country, the UN, fucking FEMA, fucking religious police—all one. They failed us. So I wandered.

Raj returns as Meena's lover in New Orleans and goes back to the mattress. Meena joins him.

RAJ. And wandering toward your nowhere was better than staying here?

MEENA. Yes.

RAJ. Why?

MEENA. I didn't want to surrender.

RAJ. But you already have. I can see you, from where I am. I can hear you, feel you.

MEENA. You can?

RAJ. Yes. I see it all, and I don't understand you.

MEENA. It doesn't bother me now. I'm not really afraid anymore.

RAJ. What's different?

MEENA. Your absence.

RAJ. I'm still here.

MEENA. But you're not with me anymore.

RAJ. You don't console me.

MEENA. I don't care to. I can't. I have nothing left inside of me to offer to you. I gave all I had.

RAJ. You left me to die.

MEENA. And you left me to die when you saw me in that cinema house back home, approached me, spoke to me, touched me, kissed me, fucked me . . . loved me, and let me go out into my nowhere. That's when you left me to die.

RAJ. Meena . . .

MEENA. And despite everything you still recognize and remember me and repeat my name, without uncertainty or apology.

RAJ. You could have stayed underground. No one would have known, would have cared.

MEENA. I wanted to be sent back, to go home. No more. I didn't want it, this place of beauty, pain, memory, ghosts. I stopped envying others. I stopped yearning for a life with the past, for something wished for, imaginary.

RAJ. Why?

MEENA. I wanted it to stop. All of it.

RAJ. But it's there: the fear, the death, the dishonor, the shame. It's all yours now. You handed yourself to them. That makes you just like me. You want them to do it for you, because you don't have the honor to do it yourself.

MEENA. I am you. That's what drew us together.

RAJ. And that's how we'll end.

The End